Here's all the great literature in this grade level of *Celebrate Reading!*

Books A–F

THE PEOPLE COULD FLY
American Black Folktales
told by VIRGINIA HAMILTON
Illustrated by LEO and DIANE DILLON

THE PEOPLE

LAURENCE YEP
THE LOST GARDEN

The Revenge of the Incredible Dr. Rancid and His Youthful Assistant, Jeffrey

Ellen Conford

Anne of Green Gables
L. M. Montgomery

"Mom, Mom, My Ears Are Growing!"

And Other Joys of the Real World

Book A Celebrate Reading!

Look Both Ways
Seeing the Other Side

Featured Poets
Carl Sandburg
Rachel Field
Sara Henderson Hay

Book B Celebrate Reading!

*Anne
of Green Gables*

L.M. Montgomery

Nimbus Classics

Free to Fly
A User's Guide to the Imagination

Book C Celebrate Reading!

THE PEOPLE COULD FLY
American Black Folktales
told by VIRGINIA HAMILTON
Illustrated by LEO and DIANE DILLON

THEO ZEPHYR

Dean Hughes

Featured Poets
Pat Mora
Shel Silverstein
Jane Yolen
Judith Viorst

Journey Home
and Other Routes to Belonging

Book D Celebrate Reading!

LAURENCE YEP
THE LOST GARDEN

A Memoir by
the Author of
DRAGONWINGS

A JAR OF
DREAMS
Yoshiko Uchida

Arriving Before I Start

Passages Through Time

Book E Celebrate Reading!

MAX and ME and the TIME MACHINE
by Gery Greer and Bob Ruddick

ROCKET RACER

Children of the Wild West

RUSSELL FREEDMAN

Just Like a Hero
Talk About Leadership!

The Revenge of the Incredible Dr. Rancid and His Youthful Assistant, Jeffrey
from the novel by
Ellen Conford

The Gold Coin
by Alma Flor Ada
✳1992 Christopher Award

Mother Teresa
from the biography by
Patricia Reilly Giff

Prince of the Double Axe
by Madeleine Polland

Featured Poet
John Greenleaf Whittier

Book F Celebrate Reading!

**More Great Books
to Read!**

**Our Sixth-Grade
Sugar Babies**
by Eve Bunting

Dragon of the Lost Sea
by Laurence Yep

**The Brocaded Slipper
and Other Vietnamese
Tales**
by Lynette Vuong

**The Endless Steppe:
Growing Up in Siberia**
by Esther Hautzig

**Tom's Midnight
Garden**
by Phillipa Pearce

**Journey to Jo'burg: A
South African Story**
by Beverly Naidoo

**Goodbye, Chicken
Little**
by Betsy Byars

The Westing Game
by Ellen Raskin

**Baseball in April and
Other Stories**
by Gary Soto

**The House of
Dies Drear**
by Virginia Hamilton

The Jedera Adventure
by Lloyd Alexander

Jackie Joyner-Kersee
by Neil Cohen

"Mom, MOM, My Ears ARE Growing!"

AND OTHER JOYS OF THE REAL WORLD

Titles in This Set

Cover Artist
Leslie Cober sold her first illustration to
The New York Times when she was fifteen years
old. Her illustrations are the result of loving
to draw and having fun doing it. She especially
enjoyed drawing this cover because she likes
making inanimate objects come alive.

ISBN: 0-673-80061-X

Acknowledgments appear on page 144.

5678910RRS999897969594

"Mom, Mom, My Ears Are Growing!"

AND OTHER JOYS OF THE REAL WORLD

ScottForesman

A Division of HarperCollins*Publishers*

CONTENTS

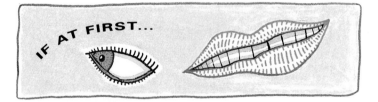

IF AT FIRST...

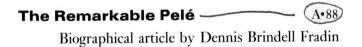

WHO AM I?
Genre Study

Heartbeats

From

Bingo Brown, Gypsy Lover
By Betsy Byars

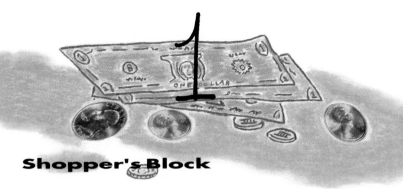

Shopper's Block

Bingo Brown had been shopping for a Christmas present for Melissa for four hours, and nothing he had seen was worthy of her. Also, Bingo only had three dollars and thirty-nine cents.

He paused in Belk's fine jewelry department to admire the watches.

"Can I help you?" the clerk asked.

"I wish you could," he answered sadly.

He stumbled on through Scarves and Belts, Hosiery, Cosmetics, staring at the bright merchandise with unseeing eyes.

He was beginning to have a hopeless feeling, as if he were doomed to continue walking through stores for the rest of his life. It was sort of like writer's block, he decided. Writer's block was a mental thing that happened to all writers sooner or later. Writers got to the point where they could not write, not even a word. Bingo had had writer's block twice, so he knew what he was talking about.

Now it seemed to him that he had shopper's block. He could not buy anything, anything!

Even if he found the perfect gift—although this did not seem likely—he would not be able to buy it.

He went out into the mall and stood watching little children have their pictures taken with Santa. He briefly considered sending Melissa a photograph of himself on Santa's knee, as a sort of comic present. . . .

This idea told Bingo how low he had fallen. Shaking his head, he made his way toward Sears.

Only this morning, he remembered, he had been a happy person.

A letter from Melissa had come in the mail and, as usual, he got a warm feeling just holding the envelope. If she had just sent the envelope, Bingo had thought, he would be happy.

Actually, after he opened it, he wished she *had* just sent the envelope. The first sentence chilled his bones.

He had been in his room. He always liked to open Melissa's letters in private, because sometimes her letters made his heart pound like a hammer.

Also, his face reflected emotions the way a pond ripples at the slightest breeze.

He had closed the door, opened the letter, and read.

He felt his usual thrill when he saw "Dear Bingo." He loved letters that started that way. Dear Bingo. Whoever had thought that up deserved a medal. Dear Bingo.

Then came the worst sentence he had ever read in his entire life.

"I finished your Christmas present today, and I KNOW you're going to love it."

Bingo threw open the door and stumbled back into the living room. The letter was clutched over his heart.

"Mom!"

"If you are coming in here to ask about the baby—"

"No, no, I'm not."

Bingo's mom was seven and three-thirtieths months pregnant, and she knew whether the baby was a boy or a girl, but she wouldn't tell Bingo or his dad. She wouldn't even give them a hint except, "It's either going to be a boy or a girl."

He and his father had a pact. "If I find out, I'll tell you, and if you find out, you tell me," his dad had said.

Then they had shaken hands like men.

"Mom, a terrible thing has happened."

His mom had her shoes off and her feet up. She was looking through a catalog of baby furniture. "What?"

"You remember Melissa? Out in Bixby, Oklahoma?"

"Yes, I remember Melissa."

"I just found out a terrible, terrible thing— she's giving me something for Christmas."

"How'd you find that out?"

"She told me. Here it is in black and white. 'I finished your Christmas present today and I KNOW—' *know* is in capital letters which means, unfortunately, that it's something nice—'I KNOW you're going to love it.' I'm not just going to like it, Mom, I'm going to *love* it. *Love*'s not underlined but it might as well be."

"So?"

"Mom, this means I have to give her something and it has to be something *she* will love."

"Only if you want to."

"No, Mom, I have to!"

"Send her a Christmas card."

"Mom!" Bingo said, genuinely shocked.

His mom leaned back thoughtfully. "She says she just finished it. That means it's something she made herself."

"Yes, yes. Go on."

His mom sat up. "Oh, Bingo, do you suppose it could be homemade fudge?"

"Of course not."

"Bingo, lately I have just been craving homemade fudge, the kind with real butter. Have you gotten my Christmas present yet?"

"No."

"Well, make me some fudge with real butter."

"I'll make your fudge as soon as I've figured out what to do about Melissa."

"I'm sorry, Bingo. I got diverted. Sit down and read the letter. Maybe there's another clue."

He sank down onto the sofa.

" 'I finished your Christmas present today and I KNOW you're going to love it. Don't feel that you have to give me anything'—"

"See, don't feel you have to give her anything. She says that herself, so don't give her anything. Your problem is solved."

"You didn't let me finish. 'Don't feel that you have to give me anything unless you really want to.' "

"Well, you don't really want to."

"Oh, Mom!" Bingo scanned the letter, looking for clues. He muttered to himself, "Let's see. . . . She's joined a club—the Rangerettes. . . . She's got a new cat—Buffo. . . . She and her best friend are reading a book called *Gypsy Lover*, and every time they get to a good part, she thinks of—" Bingo broke off.

"Well, don't leave me in suspense. Who does she think of when she and her friend get to the good parts of *Gypsy Lover?*"

"No one. It's no one you know."

"Try me. I know a lot of people."

Bingo folded the letter up and put it back in the envelope in a businesslike way.

"Anyway, there are no hints about the gift, none at all. I'll go to my room now."

He walked, head held high, through the door, but as he got to the privacy of his room, he staggered slightly, as if a heavy load had fallen on him, as it had.

He took out the letter and, with a sinking heart, began to read it to himself.

My best friend and I are reading a book called *Gypsy Lover*. It's a wonderful book. She reads part, then I read part, and when I'm reading and I get to a really good part, instead of going, 'Oh, Romondo,'—that's the gypsy lover's name, I go, 'Oh, Bingo,' and my best friend goes, 'I knew you were going to do that. I knew it! Now read it right or hand me the book.'

Bingo's eyes rolled up into the top of his head.

Not only did he have to come up with a gift! Not only did the gift have to be something nice! This gift had to be worthy of a gypsy lover!

"Excuse me," Bingo said as he turned from the toy store and bumped into a woman. It would be unthinkable to get Melissa a toy—although he had noticed that yoyos and Slinkies were on sale.

He ricocheted from the woman directly into a girl. "Excuse me," he said again.

The girl said, "That's okay." Then in a friendlier voice, "Oh, hi."

Bingo stumbled on through the mall. He paused to glance in Hallmark, he walked through a store where everything cost exactly one dollar. He could have gotten Melissa three things in there, but, still in the grip of shopper's block, he made no purchase.

He came to the bookstore. He was now in a daze. He stopped, then surprised himself by turning into the bookstore. His spirits lifted a little.

Did his feet know something his brain did not? Was he going to buy Melissa a book? Was his shopper's block ended? Were there books that only cost three dollars and thirty-nine cents?

"Is there anything I can help you with?" the clerk asked.

Bingo expected to hear himself say something like, "Where are your bargain books?" Instead he heard these words: "Do you happen to have a book called *Gypsy Lover?*"

2

Wild Reckless   Growth

"The romance section is right over there. Do you know the author?"

Bingo shook his head. "No, I just know a girl who's reading it."

"They're arranged alphabetically, by author, so if you knew—"

"No."

Bingo walked to the romance section and stood with his hands behind his back. He scanned titles heavy with passion and lust. He saw a lot of pirates, more than he had expected—he didn't know women went for pirates. He saw enough sea captains to command a fleet. He saw English lords and Arab chieftains. He saw no gypsies.

There had to be gypsies. No romance section should be without gypsies.

Bingo reached out to see if there were any gypsies lurking behind the pirates and sea captains, but his hands never reached the shelf. For at that moment Bingo noticed something that put gypsies and pirates out of his mind.

His arms were growing! They had grown

about four inches since this morning! They were sticking out of his jacket sleeves!

He stepped back in alarm. He glanced down at himself. Nothing else about him was growing— just his arms. He looked like a scarecrow!

He bent to examine his legs to see if by some miracle they had grown too. But his pants weren't too short, just his jacket sleeves.

He looked from one arm to the other. How had he not noticed that this terrible thing was happening?

He glanced around quickly to see if any shoppers were aware of his distress. They weren't, and Bingo drew his arms back into his sleeves to make them less noticeable. He pulled the cuffs over his wrists.

They still stuck out!

When had this happened? Were his arms continuing to grow even as he stood here? By the time he got home would his knuckles be dragging on the ground like an ape?

A voice behind him said shyly, "Hi, Bingo."

He spun around, and immediately realized he could never spin around again. His arms were like weapons. The girl was lucky she hadn't been whirled into the bookshelves.

She said again, "Hi."

It was a girl from school—a new girl, but even if she had been his oldest and dearest friend, Bingo would not have been able to remember her

name at this crucial moment.

"You just bumped into me—didn't you notice—back at the toy store?"

"No, no, but I'm sorry."

"Oh, you already said that," she smiled, "—back at the toy store."

"Oh."

"You looking for a book?" she asked.

"I was...I don't know....You'll have to excuse me—I just had a terrible shock."

"What kind of shock?"

"Personal," Bingo said. "It was a personal shock."

"Most of them are."

Bingo clutched the cuffs of his jacket with his fingers and stretched them down. The bones of his wrists were still—as he knew they would be—exposed.

"I thought when I saw you standing over here in romances, that maybe you were buying your mom's Christmas present because, I don't know, you don't seem the type to be reading this kind of book. I would have expected to find you back in something like—" A pause for emphasis. "—science fiction."

He was unable to speak.

"If that's what you were doing," she went on helpfully, apparently unaware of the growth that was occurring inside his sleeves.

And his arms were growing. He could feel it happening at this very moment! The bones were elongating and the flesh and muscles were going right along, stretching like rubber bands—

"If that's what you were doing—shopping for your mom, I could recommend *Wild Reckless Summer*—this one." She touched the picture of a woman with a lot of hair on her head being embraced by a pirate with a lot of hair on his chest. "There's *Wild Reckless Autumn* and *Wild Reckless Winter* and *Wild Reckless Spring*, but my sister says *Wild Reckless Summer* is the best."

At the moment, Bingo was so worried about wild reckless growth that he had no idea what she was babbling about. She might as well have been speaking in Hindu.

"I prefer science fiction myself," she said pointedly, but Bingo didn't get the point. "Somebody told me you write science fiction."

"Excuse me," he said.

"You're leaving?"

"I must."

"You're not going to buy a book?"

"I can't."

"Why not?"

"Oh, well, I came in to look for a book called *Gypsy Lover*, but it doesn't seem to be here."

"I'll help you look."

"No, I don't want it anymore."

"Well . . ."

She sounded hurt, so he turned back to where she stood, framed in the purples and reds and shocking pinks of the romance section—the colors of passion, Bingo thought, though a person with arms like his would probably never have the opportunity to enjoy such colors.

"Thanks anyway, Boots." The name came to him without the help of his brain, and Boots gave him a grateful smile.

" 'Bye, Bingo."

"I appreciate your trying to help."

"Oh, you're welcome."

"And I'm sorry I bumped into you."

"I'm glad you did."

"Good-bye."

He would have waved good-bye if, of course, he had had shorter arms. If he waved with these arms, he'd create a tornado-like wind that would blow all the books from the shelves.

With his arms folded over his chest, his hands tucked into his armpits, Bingo started for the exit.

The Gypsy Lover Letter

"Mom!"

"What?"

"Look at my arms."

"What's wrong with them?"

"Look!"

"I am looking. I don't see anything wrong."

"Mom, they've grown! Look how long they are. Wait—let me put my jacket back on. There!"

He let his arms stick rigidly out of his jacket sleeves. The cuffs barely covered his elbows.

"So you're growing—you're supposed to grow."

"I'm supposed to grow, but all together! Not in parts! A person's not supposed to grow two long arms and then two adult ears and then size-twelve feet!"

"Bingo—"

"Growing's supposed to be a natural thing that you don't even notice. And what if it keeps on— did you ever stop to think of that? What if my arms keep getting longer and longer, because that's exactly what they feel like they're doing! Then what?"

"Bingo, your arms are fine. I washed the jacket and it probably shrank a little. Now calm down and show me what you bought Melissa."

"I forgot all about Melissa—I couldn't find anything to buy and I kept looking and I still couldn't find anything to buy and I went in the bookstore to—to browse and I noticed how long my arms had gotten and I came home. That was my entire day."

"Sit down, Bingo, relax. Your dad'll be home in a minute and—"

"I wonder if Dad's arms did this?"

"Probably. Oh, listen, we're going out to eat tonight," his mother continued, as if to divert him with a new topic. "You can pick the place, Bingo. Where would you like to go? Only please don't pick Chinese—"

"I'm afraid to eat. The nourishment will go to my arms. I know it will."

"Bingo." She smiled. "Sit down. I have a confession to make."

"What is the confession?"

"Sit down first."

He sat, his long arms slung awkwardly over his knees. He didn't think she really had a confession, she just wanted to try another diversion—as if anything could divert a person whose arms were growing! And just since he got home, they had gotten even—

"I read your letter."

"What?"

"I read your letter."

He was on his feet, diverted.

"I read Melissa's letter."

"Mom!"

"I couldn't help myself. I went in your room to put some clean socks in your drawer and the letter was right there on top of the chest of drawers, open."

"Mom!"

"Actually," she went on, "I only read the part about the gypsy lover. I skipped the part about Buffo and the Rangerettes."

"Mom!" He could only repeat her name, as the shock rolled over him again and again like waves.

She shrugged. "I'm sorry."

"Mom, just because you're pregnant doesn't give you the right to do anything you want."

"I know that."

"No, you don't. Ever since you got pregnant, you've been acting like you are the only person in the family who needs kindness and consideration. You do terrible things and then no one is allowed to do anything terrible back."

"I said I was sorry."

"Yes, but you don't act like it. If you were sorry, you wouldn't be smiling to yourself. What if I went in your room and read your letters?"

"You do that all the time. You read my letters, you read your father's novel...."

"I have to read his novel in case he needs help!"

Bingo and his mom were good arguers and Bingo felt they could keep this one going for days, weeks even. Even a year from now, if she criticized him for something, he would answer, "Well, at least I don't go around reading people's private letters!"

"Like the gypsy-lover letter?" she would answer, and they would be off.

Now she rested one hand on her stomach and smiled. "The baby's moving."

"You claim the baby's moving every time you want to get out of something."

"The baby *is* moving."

She reached out, took Bingo's hand, and laid it on her stomach. Something small and round pushed against his hand. A fist? A foot? He drew in his breath.

"Did you feel it?"

"Oh, yes."

He withdrew his hand and put it in his pocket as if he were depositing something he wanted to save. His mother's smile softened.

"When the baby moves like that—a strong move—it makes me happy. I relax. Sometimes a whole day goes by and the baby doesn't move and I worry."

"Why? Is that something to worry about?"

"Not really, but— Oh, maybe it's because I wasn't happy about the baby at first. Now I want it too much."

"I want it now too."

She said, "Will you forgive me about the letter if I tell you what the baby's going to be?"

"What letter?" he said. It was surprising how the small touch of a baby's hand could push away something like his mother snooping in his mail.

"Melissa's."

"Oh, I forgive you, I guess," he went on with unusual grace. "I have to admit that I do occasionally read secret things myself. Perhaps it's an inherited quality."

"So, do you want to know about the baby?"

"Yes, but you don't have to tell me if you don't want to. I mean, if you want the baby to be a surprise, I'll understand."

"I want to tell you."

"And there's one other thing. Dad and I have a pact—we shook hands on it—that if he found out he would tell me, and if I found out I would tell him."

"It's a little boy, Bingo. His name's going to be Jamie."

"Jamie."

Bingo's heart closed on the word like a fist.

"Yes, James Samuel Brown, for both of your grandfathers. We're going to call him Jamie."

Bingo had a moment of such terrible jealousy that he would not have been surprised to look into a mirror and discover he had turned green, like in cartoons.

He himself had been named by the doctor who had cried capriciously, "Bingo!" as he popped into the world. It was as if his mother had now decided to undo all the mistakes she had made with him. She would name the baby the way babies are supposed to be named—for beloved and dignified relatives.

She would probably then continue and do all the wonderful, loving things that she had not done with him. He would be the imperfect, clumsy older brother, with gorilla arms, while Jamie—

He bet when Jamie came in and said, "Mom, my arms are growing," she wouldn't say, "Oh, they are not." She would leap into action. "I'm getting you to a doctor. We're shortening those arms."

His dark thoughts continued.

And when Jamie fell in love with a girl in Bixby, Oklahoma, she wouldn't say, "Absolutely no more long-distance calls!" She would say, "You can call, but don't talk any longer than two hours."

And when Jamie—

"Oh, here comes your father," his mother said. "Now, don't tell him, Bingo. I want to do it myself."

"No, I won't tell."

"But I want to wait till after supper, all right?"

Bingo said, "Whenever. . . ."

One Misery,
Extra Large, with Pepperoni

Bingo's father said, "So, Bingo, aren't you going to eat any pizza?"

"What? Oh, sure, Dad, sorry."

"After all, you picked the place."

"Right." Bingo took an unwanted bite of pizza. "I'm not as hungry as I thought I was."

Bingo's mom said, "Bingo's worried because he hasn't been able to come up with a Christmas present for Melissa."

"That's one of the things I'm worried about," Bingo admitted.

"How much do you have to spend?"

"Three dollars—and change."

"Send her a rose."

"A what?"

"A rose. I always had great success with a single rose."

"Not with me," his mother interrupted.

"That's why you hardly ever get roses anymore. Now I have to save up until I have enough for a dozen." His father turned back to Bingo.

"You could get one rose for fifty cents back then. I suppose they're more now, and of course you'll have to pay to have the florist deliver it. Where does the girl live?"

"You know . . . Bixby, Oklahoma."

"Yes, that'll cost you."

Bingo didn't have the heart to tell his father a single rose might have been all right in olden days when girls pressed flowers in books and fainted at Elvis Presley concerts. Today, girls read *Gypsy Lover* and had given up fainting entirely.

Yes, he was definitely on his own as far as Melissa's present was concerned.

Bingo's dad took a bite of pizza and returned the slice to his plate. There was a long string of melted cheese from Bingo's dad's mouth to his plate, and his dad wound it around one finger and put it in his mouth.

"So what are your other problems?" he said then, licking his finger. "Anything else I can help you with? I'm in the mood to solve problems."

"No. . . . Nothing." Bingo looked down at his own pizza. "It doesn't matter."

His mom said, "He thinks his arms are growing."

"Mom! I don't *think*, they *are* growing. I can feel them growing. If you'd bother to look, you could actually see them gro—"

"Bingo!" His dad reached out and took Bingo by the shoulder.

"What, Dad? What is it?"

"I just remembered that when I was about your age, my ears did that."

"What?"

"Grew! And the darn things did it overnight. One night I went to bed and my ears were normal, well, as normal as ears can be, and the next morning I got up and looked in the mirror and I was Dumbo. I had these huge ears, huge! And I had not had them the night before—I knew I hadn't."

"What did you do?"

"Well, the first thing I did was stagger back to bed. This in itself was a miracle because I had almost passed out in the bathroom from shock— and my mom came in. She said, 'What is wrong with you this time?' She always said, 'this time,' as if to imply that things happened often enough to become burdensome.

"I couldn't even answer. I just pointed to my ears. She saw the ears, of course, she had to, but she pretended to think I had a hearing defect. 'WHAT IS WRONG WITH YOU THIS TIME?' she yelled.

"I said, 'Mom, Mom, my ears are growing.' My mother—she doesn't look strong now, but Bingo, back then she was as strong as a dockworker. She jerked me out of bed and made me get dressed. She used physical force. She could hardly get my sweatshirt over my head—that's how big my ears were!

"The day before, this exact same sweatshirt had slipped right over my head, but now it caught on these huge ears and my mother had to yank and yank and yank and still she pretended nothing was wrong.

"Of course, maybe she was pretending not to notice in order to get me out of the house so she could pass out from shock herself, in private, but . . . still . . . still . . ." He trailed off.

"So how did your ears get back to normal?"

"They never did. These are them." He turned his head from side to side.

"I know how you guys feel," his mother said, smiling. "I get the feeling my stomach's growing."

"Mom."

Bingo gave her a withering look. He wished she would learn that jokes are unwelcome in the middle of serious conversations.

He turned back to his father, "But, Dad, arms are different from ears. You can measure their growth by your sleeves so there can't be any mistake about how—"

Bingo's mom reached out and put her hand around his dad's wrist, like a bracelet, causing him to look at her. "Oh, Sam," she said with unusual gentleness, "I was going to save the news until after supper, but I just can't. I'm too happy."

"What?"

"I already told Bingo."

"Told him what?"

She rested one hand on the curve of her stomach. "It's a little boy."

"A boy?"

"Yes."

"A boy!"

Bingo thought his dad looked like a light bulb had gone on inside him.

"A son." His father breathed the word.

"Like me," Bingo said, looking from one parent to the other in amazement. "That's what's sitting at the table with you right now. A son. I am a son. The very thing that is now blissing you out is here! And has been here for over twelve years. Me! I am—"

Now his mom encircled Bingo's wrist tightly, silencing him.

"I'm going to name him James Samuel, for our fathers," she said. "We're going to call him Jamie."

Gyps

"Remember this?"

Bingo's mother was decorating the Christmas tree. She held up a Santa Claus Bingo had made in nursery school.

Santa's body was wrapped in red yarn, but beneath the yarn was obviously the cardboard from a roll of toilet paper. The cotton beard had always been skimpy—Bingo had been absent when the cotton was passed out and had had to depend on donations from fellow classmates. Now the cotton was gray and was coming unglued. The cotton eyebrows were missing entirely.

"Oh, Mom, throw that thing away."

"It's my favorite ornament."

"Then you have very poor taste."

He started to head for his room and his mother said casually, "Oh, by the by."

Bingo stopped.

His mother always said, "Oh, by the by," in that casual way when she was getting ready to pull the rug out from under him. His shoulders tightened as if to steel himself for the blow.

"What?"

"A girl called while you were out."

Bingo couldn't help himself. He whirled. "Was it long-distance?"

"No, sorry, Gyps, just a local call."

Bingo stopped breathing. He froze like ice. The only sign that he was still living was that his eyes narrowed.

"*What* did you call me?"

"Oh, nothing," his mother said with a smile. She went back to trimming the tree. "Oh, here's another of my favorites."

She held up the pinecone reindeer he had made in kindergarten. The left pipe-cleaner antler was missing, and the reindeer dangled, tilting drunkenly to the right.

Bingo was not diverted. "Oh, yes, you did. You called me 'Gyps.' Don't deny it. I heard you."

His mother hung the reindeer on a branch. She regarded it critically, and then tried to center the lone antler. "Now we have a unicorn reindeer. Maybe there's a song in that. Rudolph, the unicorn reindeer—"

"Don't try to change the subject, because it won't work. You distinctly called me 'Gyps.' "

"Well, if I did do it, I did it for a joke, Bingo."

"I do not find it funny."

"I was teasing."

"I do not like to be teased."

"Well, I won't do it anymore."

"It's bad enough that you read my mail—"

His father called from the bedroom, "That's enough, Bingo."

"Dad, she deliberately read my mail, which was privileged information, and now she is using it against me!"

"That—is—enough."

"Well, she started it by calling me 'Gyps.' "

"And I'm finishing it."

"Just because she's getting a new child," he muttered as he went to his room, "that does not give her the right to be cruel to the old one."

"Bingo—"

"What do you want?"

"Come here a minute."

Bingo went and stood in the doorway to his parents' room. His dad was at the typewriter, his long freckled fingers resting on the keys.

"What is it, Dad?"

"I want you to be more considerate of your mother."

"Well, I want her to be more considerate of me."

They looked at each other. Bingo felt as if he were being taken apart and put back together and his father had found a few parts defective.

Bingo sighed. "I'll try," he said.

"That's all I'm asking."

"Can I go now?"

"Go. . . . Stay. . . . Do whatever you want."

Bingo went to his room and shut the door

firmly behind him. The letter he had started to Melissa was face-up on his desk. His mother had probably read that too. So far, all there was to read was 'Dear Melissa,' but he still didn't want her seeing it. Somehow, some way she would taunt him with it.

Did all pregnant women taunt their children? he wondered. Was it a trait of pregnancy, like wanting certain foods? If so, it was surprising that pregnancies were still tolerated in the civilized world.

Bingo wadded up the letter and threw it into the trash can.

There was a knock at his window. "I'm not here, Wentworth," Bingo called.

"You may not be *all* there, Worm Brain, but I need to talk to you. I got a problem."

"Join the club."

The knock came again, louder. Tiredly, Bingo went to the window. He raised the window about two inches.

"What do you want? Get on with it. Cold air's coming in."

"You remember that girl—Cici?"

"Yes, I remember Cici," Bingo said.

Billy Wentworth had fallen in love with Cici one day in Bingo's backyard. He had introduced himself handsomely with the words, "My name is Willy Bentworth," but the love remained unrequited. Bingo had a lot of respect for that word—"unrequited"—because as soon as you saw it or heard it, even if you didn't know what it meant, you knew you didn't want it to happen to you.

Billy Wentworth was saying, "Well, I need to know if she's giving me something for Christmas."

"Probably not."

"Why do you say that?"

"She can't stand the sight of you, Wentworth. Why would she give you a Christmas present?"

"How do you know she can't stand the sight of me? Just because she, well, avoids me, doesn't mean she can't stand the sight of me. She could be playing hard to get, couldn't she?"

Bingo shook his head.

"Why not?"

"Wentworth, she's not playing hard to get, she's playing impossible to get."

Wentworth continued thoughtfully, "So maybe the thing to do is to get her something and then if she gives me something, I can give her the something that I got for her."

"Good thinking."

"Just one more thing." He paused. "What could I get?"

"Good-bye, Wentworth."

It was hard to slam a window shut when it was only open two inches, but Bingo managed it nicely.

A Brother's Heart

"Bingo!"

Bingo was in his bedroom, standing in the middle of the room. There was a package in his hand. The postmark read Bixby, OK. This package contained Bingo's present from Melissa.

Fifteen minutes ago, Bingo had been in the kitchen, happily reading the recipe for old-timey fudge. He had his apron on, the bowl was out. The measuring spoons clinked pleasantly as he jiggled them in one hand.

Then the doorbell rang. "Coming!" Bingo called cheerfully. He went to the door, the postman said, "Package," and put this box in Bingo's hand.

That had happened fifteen minutes ago, and for fifteen minutes Bingo had been frozen in time, unable to go forward or backward. He could not bring himself to open the present, and yet he couldn't reverse time and say to the postman, as he should have, "I'm sorry, but there is no one by the name of Bingo at this address."

Now he was stuck with this package the way

people in fairy tales are stuck with curses. If only he had sent something days ago—even the rose. Because as soon as he saw what was in this package, then his choices would narrow. If Melissa had sent him a sweater—and it could be a sweater because girls did knit sweaters—then he would have to send something as good as a sweater.

What was as good as a sweater? A blouse? Didn't blouses come in sizes and didn't girls get offended if you sent something too big?

If only it could be cookies, then he could double the recipe and send fudge. Fudge was like cookies, wasn't it? But would Melissa be ashamed to say, "My boyfriend made me some fudge for Christmas"?

Anyway, it wasn't cookies, because it didn't rattle. It was some sort of garment. He bent the package, testing it. Some sort of—

"Bingo! Bingo, where are you?"

His mother appeared in the doorway.

"Bingo, I got it!"

"What?"

If he had not been frozen in time, he would have hidden the package behind his back or thrown it under the bed, out of the range of his mother's scorn. Now she would pounce on the package like a dog on a bone, and she wouldn't stop until she had seen the gift with her own—

"The fetal stethoscope! I got it!"

She waved the stethoscope in the air, and it jiggled as if it had come alive. Bingo remembered how at the beach she had once pulled up a huge crab and waved it in the same carefree way.

"Come on! Bingo, you can hear Jamie's heart! I stopped by Mom's on the way home and she listened and said it sounded like an old Maytag washer she used to have. Come on! Tell me what you think."

She went into the living room. "Aren't you coming?" she called over her shoulder.

"Yes, but first I have to do something with this—this thing I got in the mail today."

"That can wait. I have to have the stethoscope back by six."

He went into the living room with the package under his arm. He would have liked to hide it, but the package seemed somehow attached to him. Would he ever be able to open it, he wondered, or would he carry it through life, always wondering, worrying—

"Come on, Bingo!"

His mother was on the sofa, the stethoscope against the curve of her stomach.

"There it is," she said softly.

She handed him the ends of the stethoscope. Bingo had to put down his package in order to take them. He couldn't release the package, of course, because of the curse, so he stuffed it between his knees.

Bingo hated to do that because now his mother was sure to notice he was standing knock-kneed and then she would notice the reason for the knock-knees and then she would say, "Why is that package between your knees?"

"Can you hear it?" she asked.

"I hear something like stomach noises, sort of a gurgling sound."

"No, that's not it. Wait." She paused to shift the stethoscope. "There. Try that."

He listened and she watched for his expression.

"Can you hear it?"

Ta-da-dum ta-da-dum ta-da-dum ta-da-dum ta-da-dum—

"Oh, yes."

"What does it sound like to you, Bingo?"

"Like a heart, I guess. This is the first heart I ever heard. Ta-da-dum ta-da-dum, like that."

The beat was steady, rhythmic, but Bingo's own heart began to race with emotion. He closed his eyes.

He did not understand the intensity of his feeling as he listened to his brother's heart. Maybe it was listening to a small heart that was sort of practicing, getting ready for the day when it would have to pump for real—to race with emotion or slow or flutter or do whatever it had to, to keep up with the unexpectedness of life.

Or maybe there was some sort of brotherly tie

that bound, like in literature where the Corsican brothers felt each other's joy and pain or where—

He opened his eyes. His mother was smiling up at him. "Oh, Bingo, I want this little baby so much."

"I do too."

"Now, let me listen to your heart. I've never heard your heart, Bingo."

"My heartbeat won't be anything special. It's just regular. However . . ." He raised his sweat-shirt to reveal his chest.

"That's the way heartbeats are supposed to be—regular." She raised up on one elbow. "Oh, there's the phone. Get that, will you, Bingo?"

"Sure."

"If it's your dad, tell him to come home before six so he can listen to Jamie's heart. Then stick around so I can listen to yours."

Bingo removed Melissa's package from between his knees. He had forgotten about it. The emotional moment of hearing his brother's heart had caused his knees to clamp together and the package had suffered a serious cave-in as a result.

Bingo carried the package with him to the phone. "Hello?"

His mother had the stethoscope in her ears again, listening, smiling faintly.

A girl's voice said, "Bingo?"

"Yes."

"Bingo Brown?"

His mother raised up on one elbow. "Is it your dad?"

"No."

"Who is it?"

"I don't know! The conversation hasn't started yet."

He could tell from his mother's expression that when it did start, she was aware it would be a mixed-sex one.

"Bingo?"

"Yes."

"This is Boots. Do you remember me? I was the girl in the mall—remember the day something terrible happened to you?"

Boots—this was the girl who had interrupted him while his arms were growing. "Oh, yes, the bookstore."

"Well, you may have forgotten all about this, but you mentioned you wanted a book called *Gypsy Lover* and, Bingo, guess what? My sister has it!"

Bingo/Romondo

Boots said, "Bingo, did you hear what I just told you?"

"Yes, yes, I heard."

"You don't sound excited."

"Well, you caught me by surprise," Bingo said. He began to fan himself with Melissa's package.

"It's one of my sister's very, very favorite books. She's read it so many times, it, like, falls open at the good parts. Wait a minute, I'll make it fall open."

"Oh, no, you don't have to do that."

On the sofa, Bingo's mother had abandoned all pretenses of listening to fetal heartbeats. She was watching him with one of her smiles.

"I want to. Oh! It did it on its own. Wait a minute, I have to check for the good part." There was a pause. "Okay, here it is. Are you ready for this?"

Bingo told the truth. "Not really." But Boots began to read anyway.

"Romondo's lips curled into a slow, lazy smile,

but his dark eyes, staring at her across the camp-fire, had deepened with longing.

"The music of the gypsies seemed to have deepened with longing, too, and couples began to drift off, arm in arm, to their wagons.

"Finally she and Romondo were alone. He put down his guitar and in one flu-id-ly—"

Boots paused to say, "I had to sound that word out—sorry.

"—in one fluidly graceful move was at her side. In a low voice she murmured, 'Romondo.' "

She paused to catch her breath, and Bingo had been waiting for just such a pause. He broke in quickly with, "Thank you so much for, er, sharing that with me."

"Wait. It gets better."

"I—"

"Romondo murmured, 'Marianna.' " Boots broke off to say, "Am I pronouncing that right or should it be MariAHna? That's better—don't you think, because she's a countess. MariAAAHna."

Bingo took a deep breath to calm himself. His heart was pounding in his throat. He couldn't let his mother listen to his heart now. When she found out it was in his throat, she would demand to know why. "Boys' hearts don't jump up into their throats for no reason, young man, now you sit right down here and tell me—"

He cleared his throat. In a new, surprisingly mature voice he said, "I'm sorry, Boots, I don't think that's the book I was looking for."

"Boots!" his mother snorted.

He gave her a withering glance, but, as usual, she refused to wither. She grinned and turned the stethoscope toward him as if to listen in on the conversation.

"It has to be, Bingo. There couldn't possibly be two *Gypsy Lovers*," Boots said.

"Perhaps I had the title wrong."

"No, I remember the title. You said *Gypsy Lover*. And this book is *Gypsy Lover*. If you don't believe this book is *Gypsy Lover*, I can come right over and show you it's *Gypsy Lover!*"

Boots's voice had risen, and she was punching home the title with such force Bingo was afraid the words would reach his mother across the room. It was bad enough that his own words were reaching her. He pressed the receiver against his ear to smother the *Gypsy Lovers*.

"No, no, I do believe that the title of that book is—is the title you just said."

"What was your gypsy lover's name?" she asked.

A low gypsyish voice trilled *Rrrromondo* in his brain, but his mouth stuttered uncertainly, "I— I—"

"Romondo doesn't ring a bell?" She paused. "How about MariAHna?"

"Er, I wonder if I might call you back," Bingo said.

"Well, yes, I guess so, but if it's definitely not the same book, there's no need. I can't believe this. I go to all the trouble of finding this book and calling you up and letting it fall open to a good part and reading it out loud and—"

"I appreciate those things. Most people don't go to enough trouble."

"I could just cry."

"No, no, please don't, because I have to go do a—" Bingo broke off to think of something he could claim he had to do. "—an errand. And I couldn't go do this, er, errand if you're going to—" He turned his back on his mother. "—to do that."

Boots paused.

"Please," he said.

"Oh, all right, I won't."

"Thank you very much, and I'll be in touch."

In one fluidly graceful movement of his own, Bingo hung up the telephone and disappeared into his room.

"Bingo, come back here," his mother called.

But Bingo, who sat fanning himself with Melissa's package, did not answer.

The Nightmare with Handles

It was midnight. Bingo was not asleep, and Bingo knew that he would never sleep again, not as long as Melissa's package lay unopened on his dresser.

Bingo got up and crossed the room without a sound. He eased his door shut. There was a faint click as the latch caught, and Bingo waited, frozen, for one of his parents to call, "Bingo, are you still up?"

Nothing happened, and so after a moment Bingo turned on the light. Then he crossed the room and reached for the package.

Bingo had stared at this package so often that he knew every wrinkle in the paper—it had been wrapped in a brown Bi-Lo grocery bag and there was a grease stain beside the postmark. The words DO NOT OPEN TILL CHRISTMAS went around the package like a decorative border in bold Magic Marker letters, but Bingo knew that for the sake of his mental health he had to disregard this message. If ever he was to close his eyes in sleep again—he would have to open this package and face whatever was inside.

He eased off the Bi-Lo bag covering—no sound must alert his parents to what he was doing—and lifted out the package. The inner wrapping paper was blue with snowmen involved in wintry activities—sledding, ice-skating, and opening packages that contained useful objects like scarves.

Bingo forced himself to stop watching the snowmen—this was stalling, he reminded himself firmly; he had never before shown the slightest interest in what snowmen did in their off-hours. He then forced himself to loosen the tape on either end, forced himself to pull up the flaps, forced himself to take out the box.

The box was also decorative, but Bingo did not pause to see what was on it. Like a man with a mission, he lifted the lid. Manfully, he reached inside. With trembling fingers he lifted Melissa's gift to the light.

Then a cry escaped from Bingo's throat. He didn't even know he had cried out. He turned the object over, and another cry burst from him. A third cry might have followed if Bingo's mother had not thrown open the door.

"Bingo, what's wrong?"

"Mom—"

"What happened? Are you all right? Did you have a nightmare?"

"I wish it were a nightmare."

"What is it? Tell me."

"Mom, oh, Mom—"

She wrapped her robe around her stomach and sank down beside him on the bed. Her hair was pulled back in a ponytail so the light fell directly onto her face, highlighting her concern.

"Mom, I opened Melissa's present."

"What?"

"I got this present from Melissa—" He paused to swallow. "—and I opened it—Mom, I really dreaded opening it—don't ask me why I dreaded opening a package, but it's just my nature to dread some things that other people do not dread. If there is some sort of phobia about dreading to open packages, then I may have that." He swallowed again. "At any rate I forced myself to open it and finally I did open it and I looked inside and saw—I saw this."

He held up Melissa's gift. His mother stared at it without comprehension. She looked from the present into Bingo's face.

"Mom," he explained, "it is a piece of cloth with handles on it. I was prepared for anything —a book, a T-shirt, a wristwatch—anything but a piece of cloth with handles on it. Mom, what is this?"

His mom looked at it. "Bingo—"

"What?"

"Bingo, it is a piece of cloth with handles on it."

"Mom, Mom, don't try to be funny. Not now,

A·51

please, not now when I'm desperate."

"I'm not trying to be funny. I'm stating a fact. It's a piece of cloth with handles on it. For some reason Melissa has sent you a piece of cloth with handles."

At that moment Bingo's father appeared in the doorway. He braced his hands on either side of the door. He was framed like a photograph of an unwilling subject. "What is going on here?"

"Sam, look at this. Now, Bingo, don't give your father a hint. Let *him* tell *us* what—"

"It is after twelve o'clock at night," Bingo's dad interrupted. He frowned at his watch and then at them. "You are supposed to be asleep. A pregnant woman needs her sleep. And, Bingo, I asked you to be more considerate of your mom."

"Oh, Sam, I wasn't asleep. My back was hurting again. Now!" She held up the piece of cloth, pulling it apart by the handles as if it were an accordion. "Now! What do you think that is?"

"Maybe you two like to play games at twelve o'clock at night, but you two don't have to get up and go to work at seven."

"Sam, we need your input. It's like that game show where the celebrities have to guess strange objects. You're so good at that. Please."

Bingo's dad sighed. "Well, I had a back scrubber that had handles like that—only it had bristles so that when you scrubbed..." He trailed off.

Bingo's mom said, "It could be a tote bag, if it were sewed up on the sides."

"She wouldn't give me a back scrubber or a tote bag!" Bingo said. "Now stop making fun of Melissa's present."

"If Melissa had not wanted us to make fun of her present then she shouldn't have sent you a piece of cloth with handles on it," his mother said.

"Give it back, please," Bingo said coldly. He reached for the gift and knocked the box onto the floor. A note fluttered out.

Bingo picked up the note and, without considering the consequences, began to read aloud.

"Dear Bingo, you may be wondering what this is. Well, it's a—"

Bingo broke off and folded the note.

"Well, don't stop now. It's a what?"

"Nothing, Mom."

"Listen, you got me up out of bed with hoarse cries of anguish and—"

"Not hoarse cries of anguish. I went, 'Oh,' like that."

"An 'Oh' like that wouldn't have awakened me from a peaceful sleep which I—"

"You said you weren't asleep. You said your back hurt. You—"

Bingo's father said, "Bingo, your mother is not going back to bed until you tell her what that thing is. Now tell her so we can all get some sleep."

"Oh, all right." Then he added in a low voice, "It's a notebook holder."

There was a short silence. Then his mother said, "Bingo Brown! Do you honestly expect me to believe that thing is a notebook holder?"

"It is! Melissa knows I keep notebooks and so she made this for me to keep them in. Wait!"

He went to his drawer and pulled out two of his notebooks. "See, you put the notebooks in here and here." He inserted the notebooks. "Then you fold it over and carry it by these. In the note, there are instructions, also a sort of diagram."

He turned the note around. In Melissa's diagram he wore a dignified suit and appeared to be holding a businessman's briefcase. In the mirror beyond, he saw a more realistic picture. There, he wore short, wrinkled pajamas and appeared to be holding a ladies' purse.

His parents regarded him without expression. They sometimes did this just before they exploded into laughter, which, to be honest, Bingo felt they now had every right to do.

Bingo was very grateful that his mother limited herself to, "Well, I guess it could be a notebook holder."

His father sighed and said, "Can we go back to bed now?"

Bingo said, "Please."

His mother went out the door, but Bingo's dad paused in the doorway. "Bingo, do you think you'll be getting other presents from girls this year?"

"I hope not," Bingo said sincerely.

"So do I, but if you do, try to open them during daylight hours."

"Oh, I will."

"Good night, son."

"Good night."

Bingo waited a moment, listening to see if his parents were holding their explosion of laughter until they were in the privacy of their bedroom. But the house remained quiet. Bingo turned out his light.

Sometimes, to Bingo's surprise, he found he actually loved his parents.

Byars on Bingo

by Betsy Byars

A character's name is one of the most important things in the development of the character. The name has to be right. Sometimes characters will almost refuse to come alive until they get the right name. The thing that I love most about my word processor is that I can try new names effortlessly.

REPLACE: Herman
WITH: Bubba
ALL? (Y/N)   Y
   And it's done.
   The name *Bingo* popped into my head while I was writing another book. I was on Chapter Twelve, the halfway point in one of my books. I stopped typing.
   Bingo.

I loved that name. I thought, now just as soon as I finish this manuscript, I'm going to start a book about a boy named Bingo. I started typing again.

I stopped. Bingo was already coming alive in my mind. And he was not the kind of character who would sit around and wait six months for me to finish this manuscript.

I made another effort. I would at least finish Chapter Twelve.

But Bingo wouldn't wait. Only one minute had passed and I already had his last name as well.

Bingo Brown.

And I knew how he got his name!

Bingo had gotten his name the day he was born. When he popped into the world, the doctor said, "Bingo!" Later Bingo protested, "Mom, he wasn't naming me. He probably said that every time he delivered a baby!"

He even wondered, "Who knows what kind of person I might have become had the doctor said, 'Richard,' instead of 'Bingo!' "

Things were moving fast. Well, let me at least store Chapter Twelve, I thought.

So, I put the old manuscript in storage. I got a new disk, typed **BINGO BROWN** by Betsy Byars, and Bingo and I were on our way.

When I first began to write—thirty years ago—I heard authors speak of characters who did things on their own, who startled and surprised and delighted them. My characters had to be forced into action. They were like actors who could say the lines I gave them and do the things I thought up for them to do, but they never did anything on their own. "Do something!" I felt like shouting at them.

All that was changed with Bingo.

Bingo did things on his own. Bingo surprised me. Bingo delighted me. Bingo even startled me.

I hope he'll delight you as well.

I'm awfully glad the doctor didn't say, "Richard," the day he was born.

Thinking About It

1. Bingo Brown can't decide what to buy for Melissa. Have you ever been in this kind of situation? If you could talk to Bingo, what advice would you give him?

2. In a certain kind of novel, a gypsy lover is romantic, brave, handsome, and always says and does the right thing. Women always fall in love with him. Is Bingo like a real gypsy lover? Find places in the story where he is and where he isn't.

3. In most movies, a character's problems are resolved by the end. However, by the end of this story, some of Bingo's problems are still unsolved. If you were making a movie about Bingo, how would you have it end?

Another Book About Bingo Brown

Betsy Byars introduced
Bingo for the first time in her book called
The Burning Questions of Bingo Brown.

THE DATE
from The CYBIL War
by Betsy Byars

THE NEWER SADDER SENTENCE

Simon sometimes felt he was a yoyo, he went up and down so quickly. In school he could not concentrate because he had to keep watching Tony Angotti, who was watching Cybil, and then watching Cybil to see if she was watching Tony. His neck began to ache with all this unnatural straining.

"Eyes front," Miss McFawn said again and again. Sometimes to Simon's surprise she would add, "Tony," and Simon would know Tony had been looking at Cybil and he hadn't caught him. Then he would glance back quickly himself. Cybil would be writing or looking for something in her notebook, and Simon would feel instantly better.

One day after school when Simon and Tony were walking home, Tony said, "Everybody likes me but Cybil Ackerman," in a depressed way.

Tony's genuine dismay made Simon feel wonderful. His steps quickened with pleasure. But then he began to analyze that statement, and he slowed down. Everybody did *not* like Tony. He himself could name at least ten people who didn't like Tony, starting with Simon's mom, Miss Ellis, Mr. Repokis, Annette, Harriet Haywood, Billy Bonfili. . . . And if Tony could be wrong about that, then he could also be wrong about Cybil's not liking him.

"What makes you say that?" Simon asked carefully.

"Oh, I don't know. Do you think she likes me?"

"I don't know. She's the kind of person who likes everybody." He paused, then added, "No matter what they're like."

"Yeah, there's no reason she *wouldn't* like me." He held up his hands as if he were testing for rain. "She probably does like me. Thanks, pal." And he walked on, obviously feeling much better.

Behind him, Simon followed, feeling much worse. "What do *I* know," he said, but his target was out of range.

Still, with all these ups and downs, he was not prepared for Thursday.

Thursday had been an ordinary school day, one of those days so boring that when his mother would ask him to tell her one thing that had happened, he would not be able to. He would have to make up something that had happened another day to satisfy her.

Not once had he caught Tony looking at Cybil or Cybil looking anywhere but at her papers or through her notebook, and he had been lulled into a feeling of warm security.

It was walking home, with Simon whistling happily under his breath, that the blow fell. Tony Angotti said, "Cybil Ackerman *does* like me."

Simon stumbled over a root. He looked up to see a smirk on Tony's face. "What?" He felt his cheeks begin to burn.

"Cybil Ackerman *does* like me."

"Yesterday you said she didn't."

"That was yesterday." Another smirk.

"But what happened? I didn't see her even look at you. What makes you think she likes you?"

"She must. She's going to the movies with me."

"What?" Simon stumbled again. "What? You asked Cybil to go to the movies with you?"

Tony nodded.

Simon kept staring at Tony. He could not believe it. He had known that sometime in the future all of them would be taking girls to movies and maybe even to dances, but that was years in the future. It was as unthinkable now as their joining the army.

A runner passed them. Simon heard the man's rasping breath, felt a spray of sweat, heard the slap of shoes against the pavement.

Sometimes it seemed to Simon that the whole world was running, that someone had yelled, "Fire!" and everybody had started running, with his father leading the pack. And he, like the prehistoric fish, couldn't take a step without plopping belly-down in the mire.

"There's just one catch," Tony said.

"What?"

"She won't go unless you and Haywood come too."

Simon stopped as abruptly as if he had run into a brick wall. "What?"

"You and Haywood have to come to the movies with us." Tony spoke as slowly and carefully as if he were speaking to someone with a concussion.

"Wait a minute. Do you mean *I* would have a date with Harriet Haywood?" Simon's voice was higher than he had ever heard it.

"Well, it's not actually a date," Tony explained. "We aren't going to pay their way. I was very careful about that." He touched his forehead. "I told them we would meet them *inside, beyond* the candy counter. How's that for planning? We won't even have to buy them popcorn!"

"I'm not going to the movies with Harriet Haywood," Simon said flatly.

"You have to."

"I don't."

"But I already set it up. I told Harriet you wanted to make up for overturning her in the play. You made a fool of her, Simon. I should think you'd want to—"

Simon kept shaking his head.

Tony sighed with disappointment. "Then I'll have to get Bonfili."

"What?" Simon looked up. Tony's face, honest and open, looked back at him with regret.

"Harriet said she would go with either you or Bonfili, and so since you won't go . . ." He shrugged.

Simon moaned beneath his breath. He put one hand to his forehead. It was one of those moments in a war, he decided, when the first inkling of failure comes, when that first sickening awareness that the war can be lost, that *you* can be defeated, comes and stays and grows. Grown men must tremble, he thought, deep inside them like volcanoes. He himself felt sick.

"I'll go," he muttered.

Tony clapped him on the back, almost sending him to his knees on the sidewalk. "I'll tell them it's all set."

"Yes, tell them that."

Tony hurried off, leaving Simon alone.

Simon kept standing there. All week he had been trying to prevent Cybil from looking at Tony—just from looking at him—and while he was congratulating himself on his success, he learned that somehow, without those looks, they had arranged a *date*. It was like the enemy taking the castle without the moat.

He turned around on the sidewalk like a person starting a game of blindman's bluff.

Slowly he began to make his way home. He walked like an old man trying to get used to new glasses. He tripped over curbs, tree roots, blades of grass.

It was, he decided, like Camp Okiechobie again, being led blindly to the toilets by Mervin Rollins. He could almost hear Mervin calling in his clear, young voice, "There are no daddy longlegs on the toilet seat."

And when he got home at last and sank down on the front steps, he even thought he heard, once again, the silken sigh of crushed daddy longlegs.

The fact that he had now, without even trying, written an absolutely perfect sad sentence*—I have a date with Harriet Haywood— was no comfort at all.

Simon is collecting sad sentences.

A Date with Harriet Haywood

The day of Simon's date was beautiful and mild, and Simon made his way to the mall under a cloudless sky.

He began walking more slowly when he got to the mall parking lot. His determination, which he now estimated to have the size and permanence of an ice cube, began to grow even smaller as he crossed the pavement. He stopped beside a van.

This would be, he thought suddenly, the absolutely perfect moment for his father to kidnap him.* His father could leap from the van, beard flying, snatch him up, toss him inside, and roar off to ancient forests and turquoise mines or wherever real day-to-day living didn't exist. Only Harriet Haywood, cheated out of her date, would mind. Hands on hips, eyes narrowed, she would say, "I *knew* he wouldn't behave!" He shuddered slightly as he left the shelter of the van.

Suddenly Tony Angotti burst through the mall doors. He ran across the parking lot, dodging cars as if he were on the football field.

"Disaster," he gasped when he got to Simon. The force of his movement caused them to swing around like children on the playground.

Simon's father doesn't live with the family. At times Simon fantasizes being kidnapped by him and thus avoiding his problems.

"What happened?" Simon asked. His voice rose with sudden hope. "Harriet didn't come?"

"Worse! They're waiting *outside* the theater." He grabbed Simon's shoulders and shook him to get the meaning to go down. "I told them *inside,* you know so we wouldn't have to *pay!*"

"Well—"

"And now they're *outside!*" His eyes shifted to Simon's pocket. "How much money you got?"

"Three dollars."

"Well, it's two dollars to get in, and that's what I've got—two dollars! And even for that I have to stoop down and pretend I'm a child!"

"That won't work for Harriet. She's big, Tony. I was thinking about that last night. She's—"

"Shut up and think!"

"Maybe we should just go home," Simon said while Tony wrung his hands. "Forget it."

"We are not going to forget it," Tony said firmly. He began pulling Simon toward the mall by the front of his shirt.

"Well, if we haven't got the money . . ."

"We'll tell them to go on inside," Tony said with sudden inspiration. "How does this sound? We'll tell them you have to buy something in Penney's for your mother. We'll tell them to save us some seats. All right now, let's go in and try it."

Cybil and Harriet were waiting—Tony was right—outside the theater. They were both wearing skirts and blouses. This alarmed Simon. He thought the only time girls wore skirts and blouses was to church and on special occasions. He did not want anyone to think of this as a special occasion. He began to walk more slowly.

"Now back me up," Tony said. He approached the girls and stood by Cybil. "Look, Simon's got a little problem. Me and him got to go in Penney's for a minute and get something for his mom. You go on inside and we'll be right with you."

"We'll wait for you out here," Harriet said firmly. She looked so big in her skirt and blouse that she seemed to block the whole front of the theater.

"Inside, *inside*." Tony pushed them toward the ticket seller. "You'll have to save the seats."

"But we're the first people here," Harriet said. She turned and faced them. Her hands were on her hips. "The whole theater is empty."

"Yeah, but me and Simon like to sit in the front row, don't we, pal?"

This time Tony spun Harriet around with such force and skill that she found herself directly in front of the ticket booth. "How many?" the woman asked in a bored voice.

"One—child," Harriet said through tight lips. She glanced back with fury at Tony and Simon as she bent her knees.

"One," said Cybil.

Tony pulled Simon toward Penney's. "Don't look back," he said. "It might be a trick." He shook his head. "If they don't buy those tickets—well, we'll just have to keep on going."

They went into Penney's and hid in the shoe department. Tony peered around the display of high heels. "They've either gone in or they've gone home," he reported.

"They've gone in," Simon said pessimistically.

"Let's go then."

They walked back to the theater, and Tony said, "Did two girls buy tickets and go inside a minute ago? One's redheaded and one's fat."

"Yeah, they're inside."

"Did they buy popcorn and candy?"

"No."

"Bad news," Tony said as he bent his knees. "One—child."

Simon bought popcorn and they made their way into the theater. They did not have any trouble spotting Harriet and Cybil because they were the only two people there. They were sitting in the front row, talking to each other over two empty seats.

Harriet looked back and said, "Here they come, and look! They didn't buy anything at Penney's. I told you they just didn't want to pay our way."

"Penney's was all out of unmentionables in

his mom's size," Tony explained quickly, slipping into the seat beside Cybil.

Simon sat by Harriet. "Popcorn?" he asked. "Thanks."

She took the box and began to eat. Simon watched as the top pieces, yellow with butter, disappeared into her mouth, then the dry middle pieces. When she got to the bottom where the crumbs were, she offered the box back to Simon.

He shook his head.

"You're sure you don't want any?"

He nodded.

"Well, if you're sure." She turned up the container and drank the crumbs. Then she said, "I'm thirsty, aren't you?"

Simon got up dutifully. He made his way to the back of the theater and bought a small Coke with the rest of his money.

"Thanks," Harriet said. "Did they have any jujubes? Now that I've got my braces off I can eat anything."

"They didn't have any."

"How about Milk Duds."

"No."

The lights went down at last and Simon sat staring up at the screen like a sick dog.

"You want some Coke?" Harriet asked.

He shook his head.

She polished it off and began to chew on the ice. Simon's eyes misted over, either from the nearness of the screen or the fact that his whole adult life was stretching ahead of him as a series of dates, one Harriet Haywood after another.

Tony nudged him. Simon looked over in time to see Tony reaching for Cybil Ackerman's hand. He turned his eyes quickly to the screen and watched the images waver in the mist.

"The scary part's coming up," Harriet told him. "My sister already saw this. She says to keep your eyes on the door because that's where the monster's hiding. She says the door bursts open just when they reach the cages and the monster comes through. She says it'll really scare you if you're not expecting it."

"I'll be expecting it," Simon said.

"Oh, listen, don't let me ruin the fun for you!" She nudged him.

The chances of ruining something that was nonexistent seemed slight.

"You won't," he promised, shifting to the far side of his seat where he would, he hoped, be out of range.

His Own Worst Enemy

Harriet walked Simon home. This, he felt, was the equivalent of being marched home by the principal. He spoke only two words. Two times Harriet asked him what he was thinking about, and two times he answered, "Nothing."

When they got to his house, Harriet said, "You know, I think Cybil's feelings were hurt."

"What?" He had already started to turn into his driveway, but now he paused. This was the first interest he had shown in anything, so Harriet looked pleased.

"You know, because you wanted to be with me."

"What?"

"Oh, you know." She gave Simon a playful poke, and he put his hand over the spot to protect it. "Cybil thought she was going to be with you at the movies, and then this morning Tony called me and said you wanted to be with me, that you would not come unless you could sit by me, and for me to tell Cybil when we—"

"*What?*"

"Well, Cybil had agreed to go to the movies with you because she doesn't like Tony. It was all set—you and Cybil, me and Tony. I don't like Tony either, but I wanted to see the movie. Only then Tony said you wanted to be with me and . . ."

She continued, but Simon no longer heard her. This was like something out of a soap opera —lies and plots and misunderstandings. Rage began to burn in his chest like a hot coal.

"Good-bye," he told Harriet.

"Wait. I'm not through."

"Good-bye."

He went into the house, walked back to the kitchen, and waited for his mother to ask what was wrong. His face had to be so flushed she would go straight for the thermometer. She glanced up and then back down at a cake she was icing.

"How does that look?" she asked, turning the plate around on the table.

"Fine," he snapped.

"I'm going to a supper tonight—it's Parents Without Partners— and I want my cake to look, you know—edible." She smiled.

He waited, then said, "Is this Parents Without Partners like a *date?*" He wanted to remind her that he had just come from such an event himself. For the first time in his life he actually wanted to talk.

"No, it's just people getting together."

"Oh." He waited again, and then said in a rush, "Aren't you going to ask how my date was?"

"Yes, how was it?"

"Terrible, awful, horrible, miserable, sickening, and infuriating."

She made a face. "I'm glad you had such a good time."

"Thanks."

"What went wrong?"

"Everything. I was supposed to be with Cybil, and Tony tricked me into being with Harriet. Mom, she poked me all during the movie. I *hate* Tony!"

"Now, don't be too hard on him."

"Mom! When I used to like Tony you were always putting him down and wanting me to get new friends, and now that I hate him, you're defending him!"

"No, what worried me when you and Tony were friends was that he took advantage of you and you seemed to always get the short end of the stick and take the blame and you never seemed to know what he was doing. Now that you see Tony for what he is—well, I feel better about your being friends."

"We *aren't* friends."

"Tony is his own worst enemy."

"No, he's got me now."

She looked up at him. "Do you remember when you were in first grade and Tony moved here and he sat behind you and that whole year he claimed he had gotten an unlucky desk?"

"I don't remember that."

"Every time he got a bad grade, he would start hitting his desk—you told me this, and you told me that one time you went home with him and he had his report card and it was bad and his mother thumped him on the head with her ring and he burst out crying and said, 'What'd you expect? I told you I got the unlucky desk.' "

"I remember his mom hitting him."

"Well, anyway, that, to me, is Tony. Tony is probably going to go through his whole life without knowing what he's like or why things happen to him or why things don't happen to him or what other people think or feel. It's sad." She looked at him, waiting.

"I still hate him," he said.

She smiled. "Okay, hate him." She glanced down at her cake and picked it up. "Now, I am proud of that cake," she said. "I've gotten out of the habit of cooking, and I bet I haven't made a cake in—" She paused, remembering the exact day she had lost interest in cooking.

"In two-and-a-half years," Simon said.

"Two-and-a-half years."

Simon got off the stool and walked into the living room. "I hope you didn't fill up on popcorn and candy," his mother called after him.

"That is not possible on a date with Harriet Haywood," he called back.

"Because your supper's ready."

"Good, I've got to go somewhere tonight."

"Not over to Tony's. Not till you cool down."

"No, not over to Tony's."

THE VICTORY

Simon stood at the edge of Cybil's yard, waiting respectfully with his hands behind his back. Cybil's sister, Clarice, was having a Miss America pageant on the front lawn. It was the talent portion of the production, and Clarice was dancing to "God Bless America," which someone was playing on the piano inside.

Simon had come there right after supper. He had decided that this time he would not pretend to be looking for something. There had been enough lies and pretenses. He would walk straight up to the door like an adult, ring the bell, and ask to speak to Cybil. He would then try to explain the confusion of the afternoon by uttering the understatement of the year. "I did not really want to be with Harriet Haywood at the movies."

His intention had been stalled by the Miss America pageant, but as soon as it was over he would proceed to the front door.

Clarice finished her dance. She said loudly, "I want to be Miss America so that I can bring peace to all the world through my dancing."

Applause. Clarice went back and stood proudly on the front steps with the other three candidates. Simon shifted restlessly. He wondered if he could slip past the candidates without disturbing the whole production.

Too late. A baton-twirling routine to "God Bless America" began. Simon continued to stand respectfully on the sidelines.

He looked up at the house, listened to the music. The Ackerman house was like a commercial for living, he thought, an advertisement to show how zestful ordinary day-to-day life can be.

As he stood there, he began to realize that it was Cybil at the piano. He could not see in the window, of course, and never intended to try to do so again, but somehow he was sure it was Cybil, willingly, energetically playing "God Bless America" again and again. A warm feeling came over him.

The baton routine ended. Now the decision of the judges—Clarice is the new Miss America! Simon broke his respectful stance long enough to applaud.

"Why do *you* get to be Miss America?" the baton twirler snapped. Her hands were on her hips. Simon thought this was the way the losers would really act if the TV cameras weren't there.

"Because the judges picked me," Clarice said coolly.

"The judges are your sisters!"

"I can't help that!"

"Well, I better get to be Miss Congeniality or I'm going home!"

Simon slipped past them, up the steps, and

to the front door. He rang the bell.

It was Cybil who came to the door. "Oh, hi," she said.

His plan, which had seemed so sensible, so adult on the way over, now seemed stupid. Finally he managed to get out his statement. "I just wanted to tell you that I didn't really want to be with Harriet this afternoon."

"Oh, I know that."

"You do?"

"Tony told me. He got mad and said I didn't know how lucky I was to sit by him. He said most girls would consider it an honor. And you know who he thinks he looks like?"

"Donny Osmond."

"Yes! And you know what he did? He tried to hold my hand in the movies. And you know what I did? I pinched his hand right in the palm where it really hurts. Didn't you hear him gasp?"

"I was watching the movie."

Clarice stormed by. "Just because *I* got to be Miss America everybody's gone home!" She turned back to Cybil. "And you were supposed to play 'There She Is, Miss America' so I could come down the steps and—everything is *ruined*. Mom, Cybil ruined my Miss America pageant!"

"Cybil," Mrs. Ackerman called tiredly from the living room.

Cybil grinned and crossed her eyes. "You

want to go bike riding?" she asked suddenly.

Simon felt a stab of despair. "I don't have a bike."

"You can borrow Clara's. Clara! Can Simon borrow your bike?"

"If he's careful and puts some air in the front tire," Clara called back.

"We'll stop at the gas station," Cybil told Simon as she led him to the garage.

As they started out of the driveway Simon glanced at Cybil and paused. Her red hair was streaming behind her in the wind. It made Simon think of flags and banners and bands. She looked back at him. "Are you coming?"

"Yes!"

He had a brief struggle with his pedals, and his knee hit the straw basket that was tied onto the handlebars. Then his feet and legs got straightened out, and he pedaled after Cybil.

They rode down the hill in silence. As they turned the corner in a wide arc, Simon suddenly thought that his father was missing a lot out there in that turquoise mine. It was the first time he had felt sorry for his father rather than for himself. Because in this world, with all its troubles, even if you had to sit by Harriet Haywood in the movies in the afternoon, you could still be riding beside Cybil Ackerman in the evening.

He thought again about that prehistoric creature who finally got up on his legs in the

slime, stepped forward, and found himself not bellied down but—Miracle! on a bicycle, cool wind in his face, going thirty miles an hour with Cybil Ackerman at his side. It seemed so clear a transformation that the whole process flashed through his mind, with himself the final glorious frame.

"We better stop at the gas station," Cybil said over her shoulder. "Clara's real particular about her things. Let's cut through here."

It was Oak Street—Tony's street. Simon felt his heart beat faster. "All right," he said quickly. He steered to the right beside her.

He glanced up as they approached Tony's house. He braked slightly when he saw that Tony was sitting on the front steps with Pap-pap.* He wanted to give them time to see him. Pap-pap was getting ready to cry about something. He already had his handkerchief out, twisting it into a rope. But Tony was staring at the street.

When Tony saw the bicycles, and who was riding them, he got quickly to his feet. His mouth was hanging open in surprise.

Risking an accident, Simon lifted one hand in a half wave. Then he clutched the handlebars. The thought of wrecking Clara's bicycle made him decide not to even glance at Tony again.

*Tony's grandfather

"Wait a minute," he heard Tony yell. "Hey, come back. Wait a minute. I'll come with you guys. Hey, wait! I'll get Annette's bike!"

Simon pedaled faster again, and he and Cybil were gone down the hill, around the corner, down Elm Street. Simon's smile was so broad that his teeth were getting dry. He felt he had had his victory. That wave—just a lift of the hand without wrecking—that was all he needed to acknowledge it.

He felt he had seen something like this in an old newsreel. It was so clear he had to have seen it. A victorious general came riding through a war-torn city, and he graciously—just like Simon—lifted one hand to the crowd. The crowd waved flags, shouted, wept. There was none of that celebrating for Simon's appearance, and yet the result was the same, he thought. The war was over.

Simon glanced at Cybil. He wondered if she would like to ride past Harriet Haywood's and lift *her* hand. No, he decided, she was bigger than that. He watched as she made a left-hand signal to turn into the gas station. He did the same.

"Do you know how to use this?" Cybil asked as they stopped in front of the air hose.

"No," he admitted.

"I'll show you."

Her red head bent over the tire. Her curls blew in the wind. She glanced up at Simon.

Abruptly he abandoned his pose as the triumphant general. After all, the war was over. This was the real world, and he'd better learn how it worked.

He knelt beside her and watched.

THINKING ABOUT IT

1. If a friend of yours played a trick on you the way Tony did to Simon, how would you have handled it?

2. You've now read stories from two of Betsy Byars's books. If you could interview Betsy Byars, what questions would you ask her? What of your own writing would you show her, and why?

3. Simon learns about standing up for himself, but not until he gets pushed around. What if Simon had been tougher from the start? Put yourself in the newer, tougher Simon's shoes and retell part of the story.

Other Books by Betsy Byars

Betsy Byars has written many books about young people facing new situations and gaining new outlooks from them. Among others you might enjoy are *The TV Kid* and *The Computer Nut*.

---

the remarkable

Pelé

By Dennis Brindell Fradin

Four-year-old Edson Arantes do Nascimento
lived with his parents, sister, brother, uncle, and
grandmother in a small wooden house in Bauru, a
city of about a hundred thousand inhabitants in
southern Brazil. Edson's father, Dondinho do
Nascimento, was a professional soccer player, who
earned the equivalent of about five dollars per game.
Dondinho also helped support the family by doing
maintenance work at a health clinic.

One of little Edson's favorite pastimes was to
go to the stadium and watch his father play. Soccer, known in Brazil as *futebol*, is the country's
national sport, and the fans are extremely serious
about it. When the crowds cheered Dondinho for
scoring a goal, Edson would smile and say, "That's
my father!" But if the spectators booed Dondinho
for playing poorly, Edson would clench his fists and
challenge adults five times his size to fight.

Dondinho had badly hurt his knee playing soccer back when Edson had been a baby, and this hampered his play and even caused him to walk with a limp. Edson's mother, Celeste, didn't want her children to be injured like her husband and tried to keep her children away from the game. Nonetheless, Edson played soccer whenever he had the chance.

The boys in Edson's neighborhood couldn't afford a soccer ball, but that didn't stop them from playing. They stuffed a sock with rags, strings, and crumpled newspapers and used it as a ball. Their only problem might be when Edson's father discovered that one of his socks was being kicked around on the street. If he took the sock back, the boys would have to get another "ball" from a neighborhood clothesline.

The boys had no field, so they played right out on the dusty street. The goals were the two ends of the street, and the sidewalks were the sidelines. There were few cars in the poor section of Bauru, so the boys were able to play with little disturbance until the last rays of sunlight.

Although Edson was small for his age, by his seventh birthday he was a much better player than boys three and four years older. He could kick the ball accurately and hard, he was good at hitting it with his head, and he was so fast that he could easily steal the ball from his opponents. At home, everyone called Edson "Dico." At about the age of seven his soccer-playing friends gave him a nickname too. They called him "Pelé," perhaps because he was so good at their pickup games, which they called *peladas*. Although at first Edson despised being called Pelé and even got into fights about the nickname, after a while he learned to tolerate it.

When Pelé was ten years old, he and his friends decided that they wanted to have a real soccer team with real equipment. A magazine was holding a contest in which anyone who assembled a complete collection of soccer cards would win a soccer ball. Pelé and his friends pooled their cards, sent them to the magazine, and soon had their first soccer ball.

The boys made shorts out of flour sacks and scrounged enough money to buy soccer shirts. They named their team the September 7th Club. "September 7th" was a street in their neighborhood that had been named for Brazil's national holiday—Independence Day. The boys elected Pelé captain and began challenging other neighborhood teams to play them.

Pelé, his little brother, Zoca, and the other boys on the September 7th team were so good that they devastated most of their opponents. Soon crowds were coming to watch them as they played in various streets and fields.

When Pelé was twelve, the mayor of Bauru sponsored a soccer tournament for the city's neighborhood teams. Pelé's team beat one opponent after another and made it to the championship game, which was held on the field where Dondinho's professional team played. When Pelé ran out to his center-forward position and saw that the five-thousand-seat stadium was jammed with screaming fans, he was nervous for the first time on a soccer field. Once the game started, however, his nervousness vanished. Then he scored a goal, and a chant that he would hear thousands of times in future years rose through the stands: "Pe-lé! Pe-lé! Pe-lé!" After Pelé's team received the championship trophy from the mayor, Dondinho came down from the stands and told him, "You played a beautiful game, Dico! I couldn't have played any better myself!"

Because Dondinho knew that his wife hated soccer, he had refrained from encouraging his boys to play it. But now that he saw how serious and talented Pelé was, Dondinho decided to give him a few soccer lessons. Dondinho showed Pelé how to kick well with both feet and gave him many other important pointers. Sometimes Pelé would go with his father to the health clinic and, while helping him wash the floors, he would ask Dondinho about the teams he had played on and the famous players he had known.

About a year after the mayor's tournament, Dondinho's team, the Bauru Athletic Club, formed a minor-league team composed of young-sters. Pelé and several of his friends were among those chosen for this team, which played its home games in front of the large crowds in the Bauru

Athletic Club stadium. The coach of the team, a great retired player named Valdemar de Brito, taught Pelé how to kick the ball so that it would curve, and many other things that improved his game.

At fourteen Pelé dropped out of school and went to work sewing boots in a shoe factory. In that same year a scout for a professional team in the Brazilian city of Rio de Janeiro arrived in Bauru. The scout watched Pelé play and then asked if he wanted to try out for the professional team. Dondinho said it was fine with him, but Pelé's mother wouldn't allow him to go off to live in Rio by himself.

Pelé felt bad about having to pass up this opportunity, but he soon had another chance for a tryout. Valdemar de Brito had left Bauru to scout for the Santos Football Club, which played in a city near São Paulo. When Valdemar returned to Bauru on a visit, he stopped at Pelé's house.

"Dondinho," he said, "Santos has a fine young team and the city isn't much bigger than Bauru. I'm sure Edson would be happy there. Let him try out."

Again Pelé's father was willing to let him go, but his mother wasn't. "Dico's still a baby, Valdemar," she said. "I don't want him to leave home yet. Who will see that he eats right? Who is going to look after his clothes?"

Valdemar left, but several days later he returned and asked Pelé's parents to accompany him to a hotel in downtown Bauru. "A call is coming from the president of the Santos Football Club and I want you to speak to him," Valdemar told Celeste do Nascimento. When the call came through, the president assured Pelé's mother that the boy would be well cared for. When his parents and Valdemar returned from the hotel, Pelé saw that his mother was crying. She told her older son that although she didn't want him to suffer because of soccer, she would give her permission because she didn't want him sewing boots for the rest of his life.

Pelé's parents borrowed some money and bought the boy new clothes for his trip to Santos. His father accompanied him on the train ride. Pelé later recalled in his autobiography that he grew very emotional when the train pulled out of his hometown, and that he said to his father: "The first money I earn I'm going to send to you to buy a house for Mama!"

Once in Santos, they went to the Santos Football Club stadium. Valdemar led Pelé and Dondinho down to the dressing room and introduced them to Luis Alonso, the Santos coach. "So you're the famous Pelé, eh?" asked the coach with a smile.

"Yes, sir," said Pelé, who was embarrassed when the players laughed at his answer. Pelé had been warned that the professionals might give him the cold shoulder, but as he met the players the opposite happened. Nearly every player came up to Dondinho and promised to keep an eye on his boy. Then Dondinho gave Pelé a hug, got on a bus, and headed back to Bauru.

Pelé was led to the team boardinghouse and given a cot. He liked his roommates and the food was fine, but he had a strong case of *saudade* (the Portuguese word for homesickness). He almost hoped that the team wouldn't want him, so that he could go home and forget about becoming a professional soccer player. But several days later, when Pelé had his tryout, the coach decided that he wanted the hundred-twenty-pound, fifteen-year-old player. Since Pelé was too young to sign a contract, he and Valdemar returned to Bauru where his parents agreed on a deal offering their son five thousand cruzeiros a month, which was then equal to about two hundred and fifty American dollars. This was a much higher salary than the average adult in Brazil earned.

Coach Alonso thought that Pelé wasn't quite ready to play with the Santos adult professional club, so for a while he played on Santos's one amateur and two juvenile teams, which were like minor-league teams. Pelé had no trouble scoring goals, but he was having trouble getting over his homesickness. Twice he packed his suitcase and started to head for home. Both times he was talked out of leaving by the clubhouse maintenance man.

One day one of the Santos professionals broke his leg during a game. While his leg healed, the

team used other players to replace him. But when the player returned to the lineup and it became evident that he could no longer perform well, Coach Alonso decided to replace him with Pelé.

It was late in the summer of 1956 when the fifteen-year-old Pelé was sent in for his first adult professional game—an exhibition match against a Swedish team. Pelé played beautifully, but when the game was over Coach Alonso found him sitting sadly in the dressing room.

"What's the matter?" asked the coach.

"I didn't make any goals," answered Pelé.

The coach laughed and said, "You don't make goals every day. It would be nice, but it just doesn't happen."

A few days later, on Independence Day, September 7, 1956, Pelé scored his first professional soccer goal in a 7–1 Santos victory in a league game. Pelé almost disproved his coach's comment about not making goals "every day"; by the end of 1957 he had scored sixty-seven goals in seventy-five games.

By the time Pelé's first year as a professional was over, he had made such a big impression throughout Brazil that he was chosen to play for his country's team in the most important international soccer tournament, the World Cup. In 1958, when Pelé was just seventeen years old, he traveled with the Brazilian national team to Sweden. In one early game in the tournament, Pelé scored the only goal in his team's victory against Wales. In the championship game against Sweden, Pelé scored two goals, and Brazil won the world title by a score of 5–2.

Pelé did many more amazing things in his soccer career. He scored 1,281 goals in the 1,363 professional games of his twenty-two-year professional career, which included several seasons with the New York Cosmos in the North American Soccer League. Pelé also led Brazil to two more World Cup championships, in 1962 and 1970.

In the opinion of many people, Pelé was not only the greatest soccer player of all time, but the greatest athlete in any sport. He was so popular that kings, queens, and presidents came to soccer games just to watch him play, cease-fires in wars were arranged so that people on both sides could watch him, and dozens of songs were written in many languages about him. Despite these great accomplishments, one event that didn't make headlines gave him a special pleasure. Just as he'd promised his father on the train, Pelé took some of the first money he earned as a professional and bought a new home for his family.

Thinking About It

1. Do you play soccer or any other sport? How important are sports activities to you? How were Pelé's early soccer experiences similar to or different from your own sports experiences?

2. Be a news reporter and find three reasons why Pelé became a super-success.

3. Ten years after Pelé left home, what advice might he give to younger athletes?

life doesn't frighten me

Shadows on the wall
Noises down the hall
Life doesn't frighten me at all
Bad dogs barking loud
Big ghosts in a cloud
Life doesn't frighten me at all.

Mean old Mother Goose
Lions on the loose
They don't frighten me at all
Dragons breathing flame
On my counterpane
That doesn't frighten me at all,

I go boo
Make them shoo
I make fun
Way they run
I won't cry
So they fly
I just smile
They go wild
Life doesn't frighten me at all.

Tough guys in a fight
All alone at night
Life doesn't frighten me at all.
Panthers in the park
Strangers in the dark
No, they don't frighten me at all.

That new classroom where
Boys all pull my hair
(Kissy little girls
With their hair in curls)
They don't frighten me at all.

Don't show me frogs and snakes
And listen for my scream,
If I'm afraid at all
It's only in my dreams.

I've got a magic charm
That I keep up my sleeve,
I can walk the ocean floor
And never have to breathe.

Life doesn't frighten me at all
Not at all
Not at all.
Life doesn't frighten me at all.

Maya Angelou

Children Like Marycely

by Jill Krementz

Jill Krementz

How It Feels to Fight for Your Life is a book about children who have faced, or are still facing, serious chronic illnesses or traumas.

I've included fourteen children (and you will read about one of them, Marycely Martinez) who are dealing with a variety of illnesses or traumas. However, it's not the illnesses on which I've focused. I'm primarily dealing with the *issues* with which the children are coping: sibling rivalry, overprotective parents, the importance of assuming responsibility for their medication, financial stresses on the family, religious doubts, sources of hope, ways of dealing with pain which is often minimized by those in charge, their relationships with their schoolmates (how they feel about being

mainstreamed, how being allowed to participate in sports programs enhances their self-esteem), and their struggle for independence at a time when their illness makes them more dependent than ever upon their parents.

All of them are determined to live their lives as others do. They are fighting in hospitals, in schoolrooms, on playgrounds, and in their homes. They are all fighting to live *normal* lives.

Marycely Martinez

from *How It Feels to Fight for Your Life*
by Jill Krementz

I have lupus, which means that I have an

overactive immune system. Lupus is a rheumatic disease and rheumatic diseases progress through different stages. It's basically an inflammation of the body's organs. When the disease is active it makes my joints ache and I get lots of stomachaches and headaches. I get bad rashes. I feel tired. My hair falls out when I wash it and when I'm sleeping at night. I have to take special medicine that has bad side effects like making me gain weight and have high blood pressure. One of the medicines I take is prednisone, a steroid, which has stunted my growth. If I didn't have lupus my immune system would only get rid of bad guys like infections, but with lupus my overactive immune system can also destroy some good guys, like my kidneys.

The first sign of a problem was that I had cold hands and feet because my blood vessels were in-flamed. It's called Raynaud's phenomenon. When I was diagnosed with lupus I was in and out of the hospital for about a year—mostly in. I was only eight. When I was nine I was in remission for about six months and that's when I had trouble with my toes. I got gangrene and they had to amputate the tips of three of them. I had to have physical therapy for six months in order to walk correctly again.

The nurse at school has a letter from the rheumatology department in the hospital. She also has my doctor's phone number and calls him if there's an emergency. I look like such a normal person that when I get sick inside, my friends think I'm faking it to get out of class. That's because I'm always going to the nurse's office and staying there for a few hours or I'm going home in the middle of the day. One of the reasons lupus is so difficult to deal with is because it's what they call an invisible disease. On the outside I look like a healthy teenager, but I do have a serious illness that is making me feel awful a lot of the time.

I needed some help with this problem and I got it. This past year I got together with Patty Rettig, who is a rheumatology nurse specialist at Philadelphia Children's Seashore House. That's where I go for checkups or when I'm hospitalized. She made me realize that if I explained lupus to my friends I would get more support from them at school. She was right and things are much better now. Patty invited me to join a teen club, which is an adolescent support group for kids with lupus and arthritis. We meet every other month and have discussion groups about dealing with our diseases. The neat thing about sharing experiences is that you find out you're not alone— that other kids have the same problems with school, with family, and with their relationships. As a result of going to this group I had the courage to tell my boyfriend, Tyrone, that I had lupus and how it affected me. He's been very understanding and helps me with my problems.

Still, school is difficult for me. Because my knees are weak, I can't carry a lot of books at one time. I have to have extra time between my classes so I can go back to my locker and get different books.

I wanted to be a cheerleader this year but I didn't bother to try out because my knees were in such bad shape. I have dead bone in them from the prednisone. I'm still growing so it's possible that if the dead part doesn't get bigger and the new bone is healthy, my knees will get better. I'm on a very low dosage of steroids now, so as long as I don't abuse my knees the chances are good. I'd love to be more flexible—to be able to do splits and to jump up in the air. I'm supposed to exercise for my joints and muscles. The physical therapist showed me how to do leg lifts and side lifts. Patty is working with me on this and trying to help me make exercising as much a part of my daily routine as brushing my teeth. I'm getting better at it. What I am hoping and praying for is that someday I will be able to be involved in sports or cheerleading so that I can be noticed for being good at something and not for just being the shortest girl in the ninth grade.

Dr. Eichenfield has been my doctor since I was diagnosed. I call him Andy. I have two others. They're all great. Every two to three months I have a checkup at the clinic. With lupus you have to worry about the different things that can happen to you—problems like nephritis, which is inflammation of the kidney, strokes, lung disease, bowel inflammation, brain disease, or kidney failure, which is the most common problem and usually the most dangerous. You name it, it could happen. And sometimes more than one of these things happen at once. And they have. I've been hospitalized quite a few times.

When I'm in the hospital, I concentrate on getting better and getting out. The hospital is so far away from where I live that my family can come to visit me only two or three times each week. My mother works as a glazier in a window factory assembling glass. She works five days, sometimes six. My dad is a mechanic who works on buses. He fixes school buses and works from six-thirty in the morning until two P.M. We have a good medical plan but it still hurts when my mom has to take time off from her work. Because she gets paid by the hour, she doesn't get paid when she has to take time off. So whenever I'm admitted to the hospital it's very hard on the family. It's bad enough when I have to go for a checkup because even then she has to lose a day of work because it's so far away. But she's always cheerful and she always says, "My daughter's health comes first."

Most of the time I'm up and about and dealing with the day-to-day problems of coping with a chronic illness. Some days I have a headache and a stomachache. I don't go outdoors very much. That's because in the winter my fingers and toes get blue and I have to worry about frostbite. I have to bundle up because I get colds more easily than other kids. It's worse in the summer. I can't walk outside because the heat makes me feel sick to my stomach. My skin is very sensitive to the sun so I have to wear sunblock whenever I'm in the sun. Nevertheless, in spite of how I'm feeling, I try to pretend I don't have lupus and go on living like a normal teenager. I get mad sometimes. I don't feel that I should be having all these problems.

It's been a long fight, and day in and day out my mother has always been there for me. At two in the morning she'll give me medicine. When I first got sick I couldn't get dressed on my own. I wish I could outgrow my dependence on her in some areas. On the other hand, I talk to my friends and they don't seem to communicate with their mothers as much as I do. I guess it took my disease to show me just how much she cares about me. That's one good thing that's happened to me. Most of my friends fight with their families for stupid little reasons like "Why can't I go to the mall?" My father hasn't been very involved in my disease, but he's been great. He's the one who carries me if I can't walk and I appreciate that.

My younger sister, Ivelisess, who is twelve, has none of this stuff. She gets frustrated because there are so many things I can't do—little things like jumping rope, playing kickball, or running around with her. She wishes I could be a better big sister, and I wish I could too. To make up for the things I can't do, I try to buy her things, or walk to the store with her—or talk with her.

Unfortunately, I don't have that much free time to spend with her because I also have a job. I work at McDonald's as a cashier and I help clean up. I do this on weekends and during vacations. I want to learn to be responsible, but also I want to be able to buy a car and be independent. I guess my independence is really important to me because

my mom's been overprotective in a lot of ways.
For example, I'm not even allowed to go out with
boys yet. But last summer she let me go away to
the Pocono Mountains for three days because I was
in the Miss Hispanic Pageant in Delaware. There
were eight finalists, myself included, and we had a
busy schedule. Luckily, I didn't have any flare-ups.
Even though I didn't win, I had the greatest time.
I got to go to new places, meet new people, and
experience new things. I plan to run again for
Miss Hispanic of Delaware next year. I wrote
an article for the hospital's teen club newsletter
and encouraged other teenagers with lupus to
set goals for themselves and to think positively.
It helps me and I hope it will help them.

Thinking About It

1. What parts of this selection remind you of your own life? If you could visit Marycely, what would you ask her about how she manages her life? How would her answers help you?

2. As with Pelé, Marycely's mother plays a big role in her life. Describe a typical day in Marycely's life from her mother's point of view.

3. There are certain activities Marycely can't do, but there are plenty more she *can*. If Marycely and her sister had an afternoon to spend together, what activities might they plan?

Another Book by Jill Krementz

Jill Krementz asked young people about their feelings and reactions and then wrote *How It Feels When Parents Divorce*.

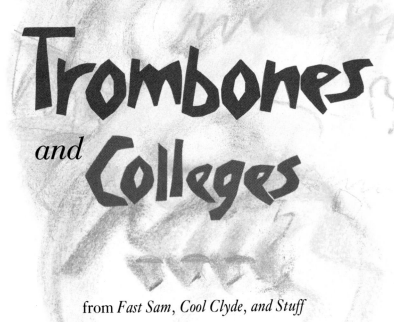

Trombones
and Colleges

from *Fast Sam, Cool Clyde, and Stuff*

by Walter Dean Myers

It was a dark day when we got our report cards. The sky
was full of gray clouds and it was sprinkling rain. I
was over to Clyde's house and Gloria and Kitty
were there. Sam probably would have been there,
too, only he had got a two-week job in the after-
noons helping out at Freddie's. Actually he only did
it so that his mother would let him be on the track
team again. Sam and his mother had this little system going. He would do something good-doing and
she'd let him do something that he wanted to.

Clyde's report card was on the kitchen table
and we all sat around it like it was some kind of a
big important document. I had got a pretty good

report card and had wanted to show it off but I knew it wasn't the time. Clyde pushed the card toward me and I read it. He had all satisfactory remarks on the side labeled Personal Traits and Behavior. He had also received B's in music and art appreciation. But everything else was either a C or a D except mathematics. His mathematics mark was a big red F that had been circled. I don't know why they had to circle the F when it was the only red mark on the card. In the Teacher's Comments section someone had written that Clyde had "little ability to handle an academic program."

"A little ability is better than none," I said. No one said anything so I figured it probably wasn't the right time to try to cheer Clyde up.

I knew all about his switching from a commercial program to an academic program, but I really hadn't thought he'd have any trouble.

"I saw the grade adviser today. He said I should switch back to the commercial program." Clyde looked like he'd start crying any minute. His eyes were red and his voice was shaky. "He said that I had to take mathematics over and if I failed again or failed another required subject I couldn't graduate. The way it is now I'm going to have to finish up in the summer because I switched over."

"I think you can pass it if you really want to," Kitty said. Clyde's sister was so pretty I couldn't even look at her. If I did I started feeling funny and couldn't talk right. Sometimes I daydreamed about marrying her.

Just then Clyde's mother came in and he gave a quick look at Kitty.

"Hi, young ladies and young gentlemen." Mrs. Jones was a kind of heavy woman but she was pretty too. You could tell she was Kitty's mother if you looked close. She put her package down and started taking things out. "I heard you people talking when I first came in. By the way you hushed up I guess you don't want me to hear what you were talking about. I'll be out of your way in a minute, soon as I put the frozen foods in the refrigerator."

"I got my report card today," Clyde said. His mother stopped taking the food out and turned toward us. Clyde pushed the report card about two inches toward her. She really didn't even have to look at the card to know that it was bad. She could have told that just by looking at Clyde. But she picked it up and looked at it a long time. First she looked at one side and then the other and then back at the first side again.

"What they say around the school?" she asked, still looking at the card.

"They said I should drop the academic course and go back to the other one." I could hardly hear Clyde, he spoke so low.

"Well, what you going to do, young man?" She looked up at Clyde and Clyde looked up at her and there were tears in his eyes and I almost started crying. I can't stand to see my friends cry. "What are you going to do, Mr. Jones?"

"I'm—I'm going to keep the academic course," Clyde said.

"You think it's going to be any easier this time?" Mrs. Jones asked.

"No."

"Things ain't always easy. Lord knows that things ain't always easy." For a minute there was a faraway look in her eyes, but then her face turned into a big smile. "You're just like your father, boy. That man never would give up on anything he really wanted. Did I ever tell you the time he was trying to learn to play the trombone?"

"No." Clyde still had tears in his eyes but he was smiling too. Suddenly everybody was happy. It was like seeing a rainbow when it was still raining.

"Well, we were living over across from St. Nicholas Park in this little rooming house. Your father was working on a job down on Varick Street that made transformers or some such non-sense—anyway, he comes home one day with this long package all wrapped up in brown paper. He walks in and sits it in the corner and doesn't say boo about what's in the bag. So at first I don't say anything either, and then I finally asks him what he's got in the bag, and he says, 'What bag?' Now this thing is about four feet long if it's an inch and he's asking *what* bag." Mrs. Jones wiped the crumbs from Gloria's end of the table with a quick swipe of the dish cloth, leaving a swirling pattern of tiny bubbles. Gloria tore off a paper towel and wiped the area dry.

"Now I look over at him and he's trying to be nonchalant. Sitting there, a grown man, and big as he wants to be and looking for all the world like somebody's misplaced son. So I says, 'The bag in the corner.' And he says, 'Oh, that's a trombone I'm taking back to the pawn shop to-morrow.' Well, I naturally ask him what he's doing with it in the first place, and he says he got carried away and bought it but he realized that we really didn't have the thirty-five dollars to spend on foolishness and so he'd take it back the next day. And all the time he's sitting there scratching his chin and rubbing his nose and trying to peek over at me to see how I felt about it. I just told him that I guess he knew what was best. Only the next day he forgot to take it back, and the next day he forgot to take it back, and finally I broke down and told him why didn't he keep it. He said he would if I thought he should.

"So he unwraps this thing and he was just as happy with it as he could be until he tried to get a tune out of it. He couldn't get a sound out of it at first, but then he started oomping and woomping with the thing as best he could. He worked at it and worked at it and you could see he was getting disgusted. I think he was just about to give it up when the lady who lived under us came upstairs and started complaining about the noise. It kept her Napoleon awake, she said. Napoleon was a dog. Little ugly thing too. She said your father couldn't play, anyway.

"Well, what did she say that for? That man played that thing day and night. He worked so hard at that thing that his lips were too sore for him to talk right sometime. But he got the hang of it."

"I never remembered Pop playing a trombone," said Clyde.

"Well, your father had a streak in him that made him stick to a thing," she said, pouring some rice into a colander to wash it off, "but every year his goals got bigger and bigger and he had to put some things down so that he could get to others. That old trombone is still around here some place. Probably in one of them boxes under Kitty's bed. Now, you children, excuse me, young ladies and gentlemen, get on out of here and let me finish supper."

We all went into Clyde's living room.

"That was my mom's good-doing speech," Clyde said. "She gets into talking about what a great guy my father was and how I was like him and whatnot."

"You supposed to be like your father," Gloria said. "He was the one that raised you, right?"

"She wants me to be like him, and I want to be like him, too, I guess. She wants me to keep on trying with the academic thing."

"What you want to do," Gloria asked, "give it up?"

"No. Not really. I guess I want people like my mother to keep on telling me that I ought to do it, really. Especially when somebody tells me I can't do it."

"Boy," Gloria said, leaning back in the big stuffed chair, "you are just like your father."

Then we all went into Clyde's room and just sat around and talked for a while. Mostly about school and stuff like that, and I wanted to tell Clyde that I thought I could help him if he wanted me to. I was really getting good grades in school, but I thought that Clyde might get annoyed if I mentioned it. But then Gloria said that we could study together sometime and that was cool too.

Thinking About It

1. When have you faced a tough decision as Clyde did in the story? What advice has someone given you that has inspired you to keep on trying even when the going was tough?

2. Clyde decides to stay in the academic course even though he is having trouble in math. Will Clyde be successful? What reasons do you have for your opinion?

3. At the beginning of the story, Walter Dean Myers refers to a dark day and gray clouds. How is that description like the mood of the characters? Did the colors in your mind change as you read the story? Why or why not? Express the colors that the story makes you think of.

The Cave

June Pritchard's family owns several trained birds, including a pet owl named Windy. One day June's three brothers, Rod and the twins, Don and Charles, go with their Uncle Paul and a friend, Will Bunker, to explore Bear Cave.

When the men were not home at suppertime Elizabeth Pritchard was angry. When they did not appear at sundown she was worried. At dusk she was deeply concerned.

She called Mary Bunker on the phone and learned that Will had come home hours ago, dressed, and gone to a meeting. "That's odd," she

from *The Summer of the Falcon* by Jean Craighead George

said as she hung up. "Junie, let's get the green canoe and paddle up there. Maybe something's happened."

June's mother usually stayed out of the male world; the feminine arts were enough for her. But when her inner timing told her the male world was out of rhythm, she could paddle a canoe or shoot a gun or get angry. June knew when her mother's troubles were big—she lifted her chin and made decisions with determination.

She found a kerosene lamp, elaborately Victorian, which she filled and lit, for the men had taken the flashlights. Then June and her mother started up the creek as the shadows darkened in the willows and the lightning bugs stepped off the tips of grass blades to show their lights.

At the second bend they found the red canoe on the bank. They hopped out and pulled theirs beside. Her mother handed June the lamp, sat on a rock, and put the paddle across her knees. "All right, June," she said with firmness, "go in there and call. See if they're safe."

June felt her mother's courage pass on into her. She hesitated only long enough to say, "Oh, they're all right. This is silly."

"We'll see!" her mother said with finality. "Never whine when there's an important job to do. Whining's for children—and cats!"

June walked slowly toward the entrance of Bear Cave, staring at the black and gray limestones that framed the opening. She dropped to her knees. Bear Cave had to be entered on the stomach, wiggling through five feet of narrow stoneway. Her fear of the tight darkness seized her as she entered, but her mother's voice was so confident she pushed the lamp ahead of her and wedged in.

When she reached the big room beyond the passageway she stood up. The light from the lamp made eerie patterns over the vaulted walls. Water rushed somewhere in the dark. In a loud voice she called, "Hey, where are you?" And "... *are you?* ... *are you?* ... *are you?*" answered back. The wind rushed out of the passageway. Stones dripped. Bats circled swift and quiet. June could feel her flesh go goose pimples. She stood still and called again.

From the darkness she heard, "June? Is that you? . . . *you?* . . . *you?*"

"Yes. Where are you? . . . *are you?* . . . *are you?*"

She watched her light create a leaping shadow on the wall and as it danced she opened her eyes wider to see the new cave-in Will Bunker had mentioned. It was black. And it rumbled with the sounds of a subterranean river carving holes in the belly of the earth. The sounds were cold and un-friendly. June fought down her urge to run. She walked to the passageway, wiggled into it, and called to her mother. "I hear them!"

"Thank heavens. Can you see them?"

"Not yet."

She dreaded going back to the cave-in; but she clenched her fists and backed up, walking slowly to the edge of the new opening. There she shouted into the earth.

"Are you all right? . . . *right?* . . . *right?*"

"No!" Uncle Paul answered. "We don't have lights. . . . *lights.* Rod fell off the rope. . . . *rope.* . . . collarbone, I think. . . . another rope. . . . flash-lights . . . somewhere."

June held her kerosene lamp high and looked around. Cached by the big boulder where the rope was tied lay two flashlights.

"I found your lights," she called. She won-dered why they were there.

"Good! Now, go . . . attic and get us that big rope. . . . *rope*." It was Charles's voice. "Don't worry, we're okay. . . . *okay*. . . . *okay*."

"Is Rod?"

"Yeah," Rod answered. "Snor toots (it hurts). . . . *toots*. . . . *toots*." With Rod and the twins and Uncle Paul somewhere in its deep insides, the cave seemed a little more friendly. She looked around with confidence before she went to the entrance.

"I'll be back . . . *back* . . . *back*," she shouted. She wiggled between the great rocks, glad to be leaving the darkness, and reported to her mother.

"Honestly, you would think grown men like Paul and Will could take three boys into a cave without doing something stupid," her mother said, angry, now that her worries were relieved.

June shoved the canoe into the swift current. "Well, heck, they couldn't help it if the rope broke," she said. "Poor Rod," she added.

"You can bet that's not all of the story. With Will Bunker on an excursion, everything becomes more than adventure. It becomes high adventurous comedy. Mark my word." She paddled hard and straight, docked the canoe perfectly in the dark, and held to the landing while June ran up to the house and took two steps at a time to the attic.

She found the rope and returned to the canoe. When she handed the rope to her mother the weight sunk her arms. "Go get a ball of cord. You

can't possibly climb down to them with this heavy thing. Throw them the cord ball, and tie the rope to it. Let them pull it down." June hurried back to the house for cord. She hummed as she picked it out of the table drawer, pleased to be part of the high adventure, at last.

They paddled back without talking. As the canoe was being beached a white shadow came softly overhead. It wheeled into a leaning willow. The shadow was Windy.

"No one fed him," June said, and laughed as she looked up to see the friendly old owl. He hissed, and they both felt reassured by his presence.

"He's not afraid of the dark," June said. "He loves it. I wish I did." But concern for Rod overcame her fear and she wiggled back into the cave on her stomach. It was easier this time, even with the bulky rope, for there were familiar voices inside.

As she crawled into the big room, a few bats swung low around the opening, waiting for her to unblock their exit. They dropped like stones and winged out the passage to hunt insects over the creek.

"I'm back," she called into the abyss.

"Okay! . . . *kay!* . . . *kay!*" answered the twins and the walls. "Now crawl down to that first ledge," came her uncle's voice. "Then call. I'll tell you . . . do next . . . *next.*" She hung a flashlight on her belt and looked down onto a broad ledge ten feet below. It was as dreary as the dark cellar—and as damp. She dropped the rope, stuck the ball of cord in her blouse, and clambered down to the ledge. There she stood, frightened to be going down into the earth. So she called to hear her own voice, "What do I do now?"

"Go to the right around the big stone. Climb down on the next ledge. We are below that." The echoes were fewer.

She turned the light on the rocks and saw another great abyss. It vaulted like a huge dome above her head and plunged out of sight below. She could feel her head spin. Her knees stiffened and she could not step. Her feet would not lift even when she took a leg in both hands and pulled up on it.

She thought of Rod and the twins and Uncle Paul depending on her. She tried to summon courage. There was none to summon. She could only step back. So she did—two, three, four, and then she leaped against the wall and scrambled back to the entrance. "Mother!" she called, "is Windy there?"

"Yes. Are you all right, June?"

"'Yes, but I need Windy. Call him to you." She heard her mother whistle the Windy call. "Here he is!" Then June whistled. Carefully, curiously, skip-hopping as he looked and walked, the hungry owl came through the passage. June picked him up, fuzzy and warm, and kissed his soft neck.

"Come here," she said and walked to the first drop-off. The flashlight on her belt found foot camps. She climbed to the first landing and sat with her back pressed securely against the wall as she threaded the end of the cord ball into Windy's jesses. Then she set the old owl on a rock and un-looped about one hundred feet of string from the ball. Her feeling of elation was rising in triumph as she called out, "Whistle for Windy!" There was a long silence from below. Water rushed and splashed in some unlighted river.

Then Don cried, "Are you nuts? Get down here! . . . *here!* Rod's hurt. We need that rope. . . . *rope. . . . rope.*"

"Call him—please!" she screamed. There was another silence. Finally the Windy whistle bounced up among the rocks. The big owl stood in the darkness and shook. He listened, swung his head around in an enormous circle, and peered into the cave night.

June knew what his eyes were doing. Last summer she and Rod had played with him night after night with flashlights. In the dark the pupils of his eyes were so large they covered the iris as they took in the light that June and Rod would never know. When the lights went on the pupils became pinpoints so rapidly they could hardly see the owl eye adjust to the light. June knew that now Windy's eyes were taking in lights of far red and of night yellow as he saw rocks and crevasses and bats. The night had created his eyes.

"Keep calling!" June shouted. And the all-seeing Windy flew toward the whistle, down past the ledges to the men at the bottom. He chuttered hungrily when he reached them.

"Take off the cord and pull. The rope is tied to it."

At her side the rope began to unwind, and reel into the darkness of the abyss.

"We've got it!" three voices shouted. "Wrap it . . . boulder." June wrapped it and cried, "Okay."

"Is it firm?"

"I hope so."

"Hope so? It must be!" The rope went taut. There was a long pause, then nimbly over the ledge below came her brother Charles, panting deeply. He crossed the next ledge and climbed up to June. "Hi," he said, and gave her a bear-hug. "Gee whizz! It's good to see you. That Will Bunker and his jokes. He had to go home early. We knew that. But just before he left we were jumping the boulders and he said, 'Try it in the dark—I'll bet you can't.' Well, you know us—that's all we needed to hear. There was enough light from a hole up high and so, dopes that we were, we accepted the challenge. We gave Will our lights and ran over the big rocks . . . jumping, laughing,

seeing as well as raccoons. Then we noticed Will
was gone. We called and shouted...but he was
off with all the lights!"

While Charles talked, he worked. "We got
back to the ropes all right. We could see that well.
And we would have had the last laugh, but when
Rod started up the rope it frayed and broke. It
had rubbed thin on a sharp stone as we came
down. He fell only about seven feet; but we think
he broke his collarbone. So there we were. We
were sure glad to hear you 'cause Don and I were
about to stand on each other's shoulders on top of
Uncle Paul's to get one of us over the sheer drop.
And there might have been two more busted
collarbones."

As June held the flashlight he finished a mountain climber's sling out of the broken rope to put
under Rod, tied a flashlight onto his belt, and
disappeared over the ledge. With a few shouts
and exclamations they hoisted Rod. They lifted
him to the big room. June followed and sat down
beside him.

"How are you?" she asked.

"Okay now," Rod said with a grin. "Let's go!"

When they were all out of the cave, Rod
curled up in the bottom of the canoe, and the ex-
pedition pushed off for home.

"Windy," Charles said. "Where's Windy?"
There was a hiss in the willow and the owl swung
down to his shoulder. Charles promised him a big

fresh starling as soon as they reached home.

Their uncle took Rod to the doctor while Aunt Helen and June fixed fresh sheets on his cot. Then everyone waited for him in the warm kitchen, and they talked of the rope and Will and the lights. Finally Charles said to June in honest awe, "Whatever made you think of getting Windy?"

June was sitting on the table. She looked at her brother to say, "a stroke of genius." But the words would not come out. Instead she blurted, "I was too scared to move. I had to!" Fear was not a virtue in her brother's world, and she waited for the teasing she felt she deserved.

But Don surprised her, "That's all right. It was a *great* idea. It's good to be afraid if it makes you think . . . and you sure did!"

"Well, Windy made me think too. I see what you mean by a well-trained bird. I'll work harder with Zander."*

The twins grinned at her in pleasure. She was a heroine in her brothers' eyes. And it was pleasant—just awfully pleasant and rewarding.

*the falcon that June is trying to train

Pulling It All Together

1. In a realistic adventure story such as "The Cave," see the setting in your mind as you follow the action. See the cave entrance, the big room, the passageway, and what is beyond. Diagram or describe the setting.

2. Characters and settings seem real in modern realistic fiction. How are Clyde, his mother, and June Pritchard like people you know? How are Betsy Byars's characters Bingo Brown and Simon like people you know?

3. The young people in this book are discussing growing up. What do they say? What do you add?

Another Book About Growing Up

In *Polly Panic*, by Mary Francis Shura, Polly
has to deal with a new school, a bully,
and the snobbish attitude of her former best friend.
Why wouldn't Polly panic?

Books To Enjoy

Good-bye, Chicken Little
by Betsy Byars, Harper, 1979

Jimmy Little's life is complicated enough, but when Uncle Pete drowns, he feels responsible for the death. Will Jimmy's life ever make sense again?

The Facts and Fictions of Minna Pratt
by Patricia MacLachlan, Harper, 1988

Why isn't Minna's home more like Lucas's— tidy, formal, organized? Well, maybe his *is* a tiny bit dull. Can Minna ever appreciate her own loving but disorganized family?

The Summer of the Swans
by Betsy Byars, Viking, 1970

Sara doesn't understand herself; her emotions seem so unpredictable and undependable. When her brother disappears, though, she learns that some people—even one person she didn't like—*are* dependable.

Last Summer with Maizon
by Jacqueline Woodson, Delacorte, 1990

Maizon and Margaret are best friends who live on the same block in Brooklyn. Neither expected the summer to bring such changes in their lives.

Orp
by Suzy Kline, Putnam, 1989

Orville Rudemeyer Pygenski, Junior, hates his name and figures there *must* be other kids who hate their names too. So he starts the "I Hate My Name Club" and is really surprised by those who join!

In Charge: A Complete Handbook for Kids with Working Parents
by Kathy S. Kyte, Knopf, 1983

Sometimes your parents are both working. Sometimes they just can't be home with you. This book gives ideas for planning for those times when you are home alone and tips on dealing with crises and other events that may occur.

LITERARY TERMS

Characterization *Characterization* is how an author creates a character. Authors may tell you directly about a character, they may let a character speak for himself or herself, or they may show what the character is like just by what the character does. In "Heartbeats," you learn about Bingo by watching him struggle. He worries that he won't think of a suitable present for Melissa. His desire to do something nice in return for Melissa's generosity shows the kind of person he is.

Irony *Irony* is a contrast between what appears to be and what really is. Authors sometimes use verbal irony to create humor in a story. The humor comes from the contrast between what is said and what is meant. In "The Date," Harriet tells Simon the plot of the movie they will see, and then says, ". . . don't let me ruin the fun for you." Simon's reply, "You won't," is an example of irony. She couldn't possibly ruin his fun since he hadn't planned on having any, and she has already ruined the movie for him by telling him the surprise parts.

Mood   *Mood* is the feeling of a piece. Sometimes it reflects the way characters feel. The mood at the beginning of "Trombones and Colleges" is sad. The first line gives you a clue: "It was a dark day when we got our report cards." At the end, Clyde, the main character, resolves his problem. Did you feel the mood lighten? Did you sense a happier mood?

Narrative Nonfiction   A narrative is a story. *Narrative nonfiction* tells about a true event or a series of events that happened, often in the order in which they occurred. "The Remarkable Pelé," a biography, is an example of narrative nonfiction.

Realistic Fiction   *Realistic fiction* is a story that could really happen; the characters act and sound like real people. In modern realistic fiction, the story takes place in the present. The stories "Heartbeats" and "The Date" are examples of modern realistic fiction. Bingo Brown and Simon behave like people you might know.

Theme   *Theme* is the important idea or central meaning of the story. Sometimes it's the lesson behind the story, and the author tells you directly what that lesson is. Sometimes the theme isn't directly stated, and you are supposed to figure the theme out for yourself. "Keep on trying even if things don't seem to be going your way" could be a theme for "Trombones and Colleges." Do you agree?

GLOSSARY

Vocabulary from your selections

a bil i ty (ə bil′ə tē), **1** power to do or act:
A horse has the ability to work.
2 power to do some special thing; skill:
He has great ability in making jewelry.
3 special natural gift; talent: *Musical
ability often shows itself early in life.*
n., pl. **a bil i ties.**

a byss (ə bis′), **1** a bottomless or very
great depth; a very deep crack in the
earth: *The mountain climber stood at
the edge of a cliff overlooking an abyss
four thousand feet deep.* **2** anything
too deep or great to be measured;
lowest depth: *an abyss of despair. n.,
pl.* **a byss es.**

ac a dem ic (ak′ə dem′ik), **1** of schools,
colleges, and their studies: *The academic year begins when school opens in
September.* **2** concerned with general
education rather than commercial,
technical, or professional education:
*History and French are academic
subjects; typewriting and bookkeeping
are commercial subjects. adj.*

ac com plish ment (ə kom′plish mənt),
1 something that has been done
with knowledge, skill, or ability;
achievement: *The teachers were proud
of their pupils' accomplishments.*
2 skill in some social art or grace: *She
was a person of many accomplishments;
she could play the guitar, paint a picture, and change a tire equally well. n.*

an guish (ang′gwish), very great pain or
grief; great distress: *He was in anguish
until the doctor set his broken leg. n.*

anguish

A • 140

com mer cial (kə mėr′shəl), **1** having to do with trade or business: *a store or other commercial establishment.* **2** made to be sold for a profit: *Anything you can buy in a store is a commercial product.* **3** an advertising message on radio or television, broadcast between or during programs. 1,2 *adj.*, 3 *n.* —**com mer′cial ly,** *adv.*

cord (kôrd), **1** a thick string; very thin rope: *She tied the package with a cord.* **2** fasten or tie up with a cord: *They corded bundles of papers.* 1 *n.*, 2 *v.* —**cord′like′,** *adj.*

dis prove (dis pruv′), prove false or incorrect: *She disproved her brother's claim that he had less candy by weighing both boxes.* *v.,* **dis proved, dis prov ing.**

doc u ment (dok′yə mənt *for 1;* dok′yə ment *for 2*), **1** something written or printed that gives information or proof of some fact; any object used as evidence. Letters, maps, and pictures are documents. **2** prove or support by means of documents or the like: *Can you document your theory with facts?* 1 *n.*, 2 *v.*

e quiv a lent (i kwiv′ə lənt), **1** equal; the same in value, force, effect, meaning, etc.: *Nodding your head is equivalent to saying yes.* **2** something equivalent: *Five pennies are the equivalent of a nickel.* 1 *adj.*, 2 *n.*

immune system (i myün′ sis′təm), system of antibodies and special white blood cells in a person or animal that recognize, attack, and destroy germs and other foreign material that enter the body. *n.*

in de pend ence (in′di pen′dəns), condition of being free; freedom from the control, influence, support, or help of others: *The American colonies won independence from England.* *n.*

a	hat	oi	oil
ā	age	ou	out
ä	far	u	cup
e	let	ù	put
ē	equal	ü	rule
ėr	term		
i	it	ch	child
ī	ice	ng	long
o	hot	sh	she
ō	open	th	thin
ô	order	ᴛʜ	then
		zh	measure

ə = {
a in about
e in taken
i in pencil
o in lemon
u in circus
}

cord (def. 1)

jess

in·flam·ma·tion (in′flə mā′shən), a diseased condition of some part of the body, marked by heat, redness, swelling, and pain: *A boil is an inflammation of the skin. n.*

in·fur·i·ate (in fyür′ē āt), fill with wild, fierce anger; make furious; enrage: *Their insults infuriated him. v.,* **in·fur·i·at·ed, in·fur·i·at·ing.**

jess (jes), **1** a short strap fastened around a falcon's leg, to which a leash can be attached. **2** put jesses on. **1** *n.,* **2** *v.*

lull (lul), **1** soothe with sounds or caresses; cause to sleep: *The soft music lulled me to sleep.* **2** make or become calm or more nearly calm; quiet: *Their confidence lulled my fears. The wind lulled.* **3** period of less noise or violence; brief calm: *a lull in a storm.* **1,2** *v.,* **3** *n.*

non·ex·ist·ent (non′ig zis′tənt), does not exist; is not. *adj.*

op·por·tu·ni·ty (op′ər tü′nə tē *or* op′ər tyü′nə tē), a good chance; favorable time; convenient occasion: *I have had no opportunity to give him your message. n., pl.* **op·por·tu·ni·ties.**

o·ver·pro·tec·tive, *See* protective.

pes·si·mis·tic (pes′ə mis′tik), **1** inclined to look on the dark side of things or to see all the difficulties and disadvantages. **2** expecting the worst: *I was pessimistic about passing the test because I hadn't studied. adj.*

pho·bi·a (fō′bē ə), a deep, irrational fear of a certain thing or group of things: *a phobia about snakes. n., pl.* **pho·bi·as.**

pre·tense (prē′tens *or* pri tens′), **1** make-believe; pretending: *My anger was all pretense.* **2** a false appearance: *Under pretense of dropping a pencil, she looked at a classmate's test.* **3** a false claim: *She made a pretense of knowing our secret. n. Also,* **pretence.**

pro tec tive (prə tek′tiv), being a defense; protecting: *the hard protective covering of a turtle. The bear was protective of its cubs. adj.*

re mis sion (ri mish′ən), a lessening or disappearance (of pain, symptoms, force, labor, etc.): *The storm continued without remission. n.*

re quite (ri kwīt′), pay back; make return for: *requite kindness with love. v.*, **re quit ed, re quit ing.** —**re quit′er,** *n.*

sat is fac tor y (sat′i sfak′tər ē), satisfying; good enough to satisfy; pleasing or adequate. *adj.*

spec ta tor (spek′tā tər), person who looks on without taking part: *There were many spectators at the game. n.*

ster oid (ster′oid), any of a large class of structurally related biochemical compounds, including the sterols, various hormones, and acids found in bile; may heal or control certain conditions if prescribed by a medical doctor. *n.*

sub ter ra ne an (sub′tə rā′nē ən), underground: *A subterranean passage led from the castle to a cave. adj.*

taunt (tônt), **1** jeer at; mock; reproach: *My classmates taunted me for being teacher's pet.* **2** a bitter or insulting remark; mocking; jeering. 1. *v.*, 2 *n.*

un re quit ed, *See* requite.

vault (vôlt), **1** an arched roof or ceiling; series of arches. **2** an arched space or passage. **3** make in the form of a vault: *The roof was vaulted. 1,2, n., 3 v.*

zest (zest), **1** keen enjoyment; relish: *The hungry children ate with zest.* **2** a pleasant or exciting quality, flavor, etc.: *Wit gives zest to conversation. n.*

zest ful (zest′fəl), characterized by zest. *adj.* —**zest′ful ly,** *adv.*

a hat	oi oil
ā age	ou out
ä far	u cup
e let	ù put
ē equal	ü rule
ėr term	
i it	ch child
ī ice	ng long
o hot	sh she
ō open	th thin
ô order	ᵺ then
	zh measure

ə = { a in about / e in taken / i in pencil / o in lemon / u in circus }

vault (def. 1)—vault of a cathedral

ACKNOWLEDGMENTS

Text

Page 6: "Heartbeats" from *Bingo Brown, Gypsy Lover* by Betsy Byars. Copyright © 1990 by Betsy Byars. Used by permission of Viking Penguin, a division of Penguin Books USA Inc.

Page 56: "Byars on Bingo" by Betsy Byars. Copyright © 1991 by Betsy Byars.

Page 60: "The Date" from *The Cybil War* by Betsy Byars. Copyright © 1981 by Betsy Byars. Used by permission of Viking Penguin, a division of Penguin Books USA Inc.

Page 88: "Pelé" from *Remarkable Children: Twenty Who Made History* by Dennis Fradin. Copyright © 1987 by Dennis Brindell Fradin. By permission of Little, Brown and Company.

Page 100: "Life Doesn't Frighten Me" from *And Still I Rise* by Maya Angelou. Copyright © 1978 by Maya Angelou. Reprinted by permission of Random House, Inc.

Page 102: "Children Like Marycely" by Jill Krementz. Copyright © 1991 by Jill Krementz.

Page 104: "Marycely Martinez" from *How It Feels to Fight for Your Life* by Jill Krementz. Copyright © 1989 by Jill Krementz, Inc. By permission of Little, Brown and Company.

Page 113: "Trombones and Colleges" from *Fast Sam, Cool Clyde, and Stuff* by Walter Dean Myers. Copyright © 1975 by Walter Dean Myers. Used by permission of Viking Penguin, a division of Penguin Books USA Inc.

Page 122: "The Cave" from *The Summer of the Falcon* by Jean Craighead George. Copyright © 1962 by Jean Craighead George. Reprinted by permission of Curtis Brown, Ltd.

Artists

Illustrations owned and copyrighted by the illustrator.
Cover: Leslie Cober
Pages 1–5: Leslie Cober
Pages 6–55: Lou Beach and Calef Brown
Pages 56–58: Calef Brown
Pages 60–87: Leslie Cober
Pages 89, 96: Connie Connally
Pages 100–101: Rosanne Lobes
Pages 112–121: Gil Ashby
Pages 122–132: Donald Martin
Pages 135–138, 140, 144: Leslie Cober

Photographs

Page 57: Courtesy of Betsy Byars
Page 99: New York Cosmos
Page 103: Courtesy of Jill Krementz
Pages 104, 110, 111: Jill Krementz
Page 140: Library of Congress
Page 142: Hank Morgan, Rainbow
Page 143: Folger Shakespeare Library
Unless otherwise acknowledged, all photographs are the property of Scott-Foresman.

Glossary

The contents of the Glossary entries in this book have been adapted from *Scott, Foresman Intermediate Dictionary*, Copyright © 1988 by Scott, Foresman and Company, and *Scott, Foresman Advanced Dictionary*, Copyright © 1988 by Scott, Foresman and Company.